Teaching the Christian Year

Seasons
of Faith

For Intergenerational Use

by
Marcia Joslin Stoner

Abingdon Press

Nashville

Seasons of Faith
Teaching the Christian Year
For Intergenerational Use

Credits are listed on page 160.

A special thank you goes to the following people who contributed specific activities to this book:
James H. Ritchie, Carol McDonough, Craig Bowler, Mary Leslie Dawson-Ramsey,
JoAnne Chase, Karen Sledge, James Wrede, and Karen Young.

05 06 07 08 09 10 11 12 — 10 9 8 7 6 5 4 3 2

MANUFACTURED IN THE UNITED STATES OF AMERICA

Table of contents

How to Use This Book

The activities in this book have been separated into categories. However, keep in mind that activities can be modified for other lessons—don't be afraid to combine or to pick and choose activities from different sections.

FOR PRETEEN AND YOUTH ACTIVITIES

Information About Holidays—Share some of the background about our Christian Year before and/or during sessions on those holidays.

Additional Activities—Need something extra to supplement a regular lesson? Pick out one or two activities that are appropriate to your subject, age group, and lesson needs.

Short-Term Studies—A six-week Lenten study is provided in its entirety. For other studies, combine activities by categories and use the Lesson Plan Form on page 6 to quickly lay out a short-term study.

After-School Care or Youth Group Activities—Choose an activity to do when you want to awaken interest or highlight a specific point with your group, or plan one or more sessions around the Christian Year.

FOR INTERGENERATIONAL ACTIVITIES

Third Grade Through Adult—Many activities in this book require an ability to read, so those in the third grade and up are best suited to appreciate the activities in the entire book. Let more sophisticated readers work with less sophisticated readers. *Some activities require abstract thinking skills and are most appropriate for the preteen level and beyond.*

Kindergarten Through Adult—Choose non-reading-oriented activities and let older children, youth, or adults help the younger children.

FOR SHORT-TERM INTERGENERATIONAL STUDIES

Use the Lesson Plan Form on page 6 to set up short-term sessions about the Christian Year. Try to form intergenerational groups that contain members of every age level.

The six-week Lenten study is perfect for intergenerational use, especially fifth grade through adult.

FOR CHURCH SETTING OR HOME WORSHIP

A reproducible Advent & Christmas Worship Booklet is provided for church or family use.

Sample Lesson Plan

*This sample lesson plan is based on one possible way a class could use this book
for a Christmas lesson. Working with the mission project would require more than one session.*

SESSION TIME 2 hours

ARRIVAL ACTIVITY: Christian Christmas Tree, p. 48
Supplies to gather: artificial Christmas tree and stand, tree skirt, scissors, glue, paper
Supplies to get / things to do: photocopy patterns on pages 49-52; buy felt, colorful trim, foam board, and ornament hooks.

OPENING ACTIVITY: Read today's Bible Story: Matthew 1:18-25
Supplies to gather: Bibles
Supplies to get / things to do:

MAIN ACTIVITY: Create a Gameboard, p. 32
Supplies to gather: Bibles, tape, scissors, construction paper, colored felt-tip markers, index cards
Supplies to get / things to do: photocopy gameboard layout (p. 33); buy several large sheets of posterboard.

GAME: Listen to Me, p. 39
Supplies to gather: blindfold
Supplies to get / things to do:

CRAFT: Stained-Glass Nativity, pp. 14 & 15
Supplies to gather: clear plastic soft drink bottles, scissors, small paintbrushes, pens, tape, matches
Supplies to get / things to do: buy carbon paper, utility knife, plaster of Paris, votive candle, and 3-D paints; photocopy patterns on pages 16-21.

MISSIONS: Decide as a group
Supplies to gather: information on several possible mission projects
Supplies to get / things to do: call Judy J., mission chair, for help

MUSIC: Combine with worship
Supplies to gather: Tom B. (make sure piano is in place for him)
Supplies to get / things to do: ask youth to carry hymnals from sanctuary to classroom.

WORSHIP: Use Advent & Christmas Worship Booklet, pp. 25-30
Supplies to gather: Advent wreath, candles, matches.
Supplies to get / things to do: photocopy worship booklets and put them together. (Ask youth to help.)

What have I forgotten?

Lesson Plan Form

SESSION TIME _____

ARRIVAL ACTIVITY: _____
Supplies to gather: _____
Supplies to get / things to do: _____
_____

OPENING ACTIVITY: _____
Supplies to gather: _____
Supplies to get / things to do: _____
_____

MAIN ACTIVITY: _____
Supplies to gather: _____
Supplies to get / things to do: _____
_____

GAME: _____
Supplies to gather: _____
Supplies to get / things to do: _____
_____

CRAFT: _____
Supplies to gather: _____
Supplies to get / things to do: _____
_____

MISSIONS: _____
Supplies to gather: _____
Supplies to get / things to do: _____
_____

MUSIC: _____
Supplies to gather: _____
Supplies to get / things to do: _____
_____

WORSHIP: _____
Supplies to gather: _____
Supplies to get / things to do: _____
_____

What have I forgotten? _____
_____
_____
_____

Seasons of Faith

Celebrating the Christian Year

Christians experience God through the events of history. It is through God acting in history that God is made known to us: by the calling of Abraham to be a people, by Moses leading the Israelites from slavery into the Promised Land, and by God Incarnate reaching out once again for the salvation of humankind.

This makes time very important to the Christian faith. It is because of this that the cycle of the Christian Year is what grounds our relationship with God.

The foundation of our relationship with God is the Lord's Day—Sunday. See Acts 20:7; 1 Corinthians 16:2; and Revelation 1:10 for confirmation that the first Christians celebrated the Lord's Day. Of course the concept of the Lord's Day goes clear back to Genesis, when God created the world and rested on the seventh day. For Christians the celebration of that seventh day became the celebration of the day Christ was resurrected—when God made himself known through Jesus Christ.

The Christian Year has evolved through the original relationship with the Lord's Day as a celebration of the life and resurrection of Jesus. The Christian Year is designed as a commemoration of the life of Jesus, our Lord, and as a way to more fully comprehend what Jesus' Lordship means.

This book will help you celebrate the days of the Christian Year; at the end it offers a few suggestions for giving some other holidays a special Christian focus.

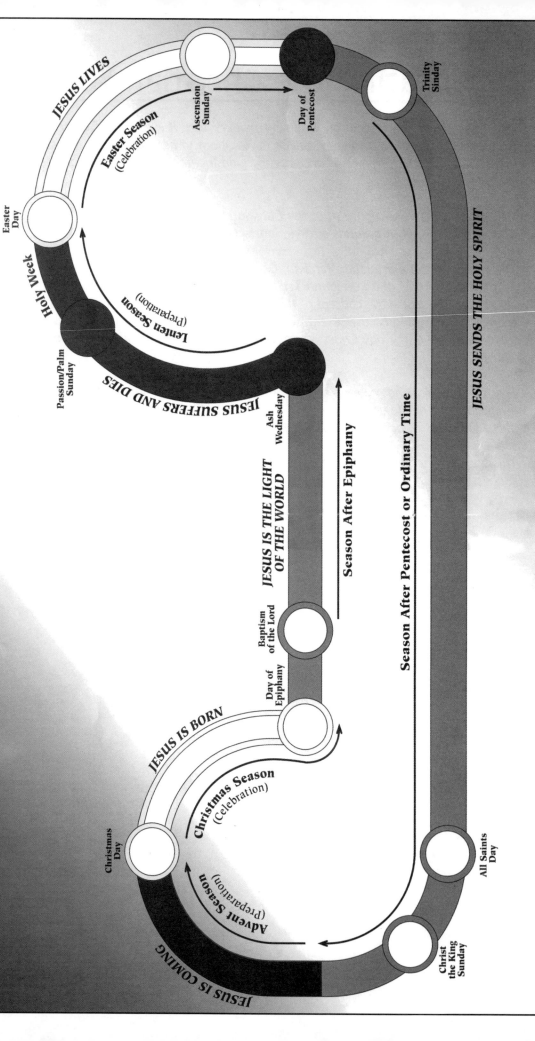

Colors of the Christian Year

Season	Color
Advent	purple or blue
Christmas (Christmas Eve through Epiphany)	white or gold
Season After The Epiphany (Ordinary Time)	green
exceptions are First Sunday After the Epiphany (The Lord's Baptism) Last Sunday of Ordinary Time (The Transfiguration)	 white white
Lent	purple
Holy Week except Holy Thursday, Good Friday, Holy Saturday	red no color
Easter Season	white or gold
Day Of Pentecost	red
Season After Pentecost (Ordinary Time or Kingdomtide)	green
exceptions are **First Sunday After Pentecost** (Trinity Sunday) **All Saints Day** **Thanksgiving** **Christ the King Sunday**	 white white red or white white

Calendar for Dating Easter and Related Holy Days

Year	Ash Wednesday	Easter Day	Day of Pentecost	First Sunday of Advent
2004	February 25	April 11	May 30	November 28
2005	February 9	March 27	May 15	November 27
2006	March 1	April 16	June 4	December 3
2007	February 21	April 8	May 27	December 2
2008	February 6	March 23	May 11	November 30
2009	February 25	April 12	May 31	November 29
2010	February 17	April 4	May 23	November 28
2011	March 9	April 24	June 12	November 27
2012	February 22	April 8	May 27	December 2
2013	February 13	March 31	May 19	December 1
2014	March 5	April 20	June 8	November 30
2015	February 18	April 5	May 24	November 29
2016	February 10	March 27	May 15	November 27
2017	March 1	April 16	June 4	December 3
2018	February 14	April 1	May 20	December 2
2019	March 6	April 21	June 9	December 1
2020	February 26	April 12	May 31	November 29

Advent
Christmas
Epiphany

Advent

Advent is the beginning of the Christian Year—the start of one of the most powerful seasons of the year. It is rich with symbolism. Advent is a season that is emphasized more by Western Christians than by Eastern Christians.

The Advent season is observed for the four weeks preceding Christmas. It has historically been seen as a time of penance, anticipation, and preparation. It is a time when Christians are to prepare their hearts for a great event. It celebrates the gift of Christ to God's people. In its beginnings it was seen as a time when Christians concentrated on the anticipated second coming of Christ. It also held the expectation that we were to share in the Kingdom.

Advent has been celebrated at least since the sixth century, when it appears to have been made into the beginning of the Christian Year.

The Advent, Christmas, and Epiphany seasons, like Easter and Pentecost, have traditionally been times when baptism has held great importance.

Many people have made Advent a time of frenetic activities—buying large numbers of gifts, baking enormous amounts of cookies, and running themselves ragged. While preparing to celebrate is certainly an appropriate response to the anticipated coming of God Incarnate, the true meaning of Advent is inward reflection, penance, and preparing our souls to meet Christ, the Redeemer.

The activities and excitement surrounding the Advent season give us unique opportunities to enrich the lives of our family, providing traditions and memories that bond a family together while at the same time giving opportunities for family members to enrich their spiritual lives. At home around the Advent wreath is one of the few times some modern families will set aside to worship together.

Advent concentrates on the biblical stories leading up to the birth of Jesus and the messianic prophecies:

- *The announcement to Joseph of the impending birth of the Messiah—Matthew 1:18-25*
- *The announcement to Mary of the impending birth of the Messiah—Luke 1:26-38*
- *Mary's visit to her cousin Elizabeth—Luke 1:39-56*
- *The trip of Mary and Joseph to be registered in Bethlehem—Luke 2:1-7*

Prophecy Comparison Chart

Old and New Testament Prophecy of Christ's Birth

Old Testament		New Testament
Psalm 89:3-4, 35-37 2 Samuel 7:12-13 Isaiah 11:1-9	The Messiah will be a descendant of David	Matthew 22:41-45 Mark 12:36 Luke 20:41-43 John 7:40-43 Matthew 1:1-17
Isaiah 7:14	The Messiah will be born of a virgin	Matthew 1:23 Luke 1:34
Micah 5:2 1 Samuel 16:3-4	The Messiah will come from Bethlehem	Matthew 2:4-6 Luke 2:11 (David's hometown was Bethlehem, so Bethlehem became known as "The City of David.")
Hosea 11:1	The flight to Egypt	Matthew 2:15

Activity: Stained-Glass Nativity

This activity will take more than one session to complete as paints must dry. You might want to work on this Nativity set throughout the Advent season. This makes a wonderful group project because each person or small group can work on a different Nativity figure.

You will need:

carbon paper	tape
pencil or pen	3-D paint
multiple colors of stained-glass paint	small paintbrushes
scissors	tea-light candle in metal cup (one for each figure)
plaster of Paris	matches
utility knife	

two- or three-liter clear soft drink bottles (one for each figure you choose to do—number depends upon how many figures, such as shepherds, you want in your Nativity set)

1. Begin gathering soft-drink bottles weeks in advance.

2. Make photocopies of the patterns on pages 16 through 21.

3. Remove the label from the soft-drink bottle. (You'll be working on the opposite side of the bottle from the label. The part where glue and/or a portion of the label remains will eventually be cut away, so don't worry about getting all of it off.)

4. Transfer the pattern to the bottle using a piece of carbon paper. Tape the pattern and the carbon paper to the bottle to hold it in place. Use a pencil or pen and draw over each line, pressing firmly to make sure it leaves a dark impression.

5. To create the appearance of the lead that holds pieces of glass together in a real stained-glass window, use 3-D paint—available through any craft store or supplier—to outline the pattern. Squirt the paint directly from the bottle onto the pattern, being careful not to let the lines become too wide.

6. Set the soft-drink bottle in a safe place until completely dry. (This takes quite a while.)

7. When bottle is completely dry add the stained-glass paints. The outline you made with 3-D paints will provide little "reservoirs" for the paint, making it relatively easy to apply the stained-glass paints.

Refer to your pattern for the suggested color for each section of the figure. Apply the paint evenly to each section. Be sure to wash out the brush between colors. When finished set it aside to dry completely. (This will take a while.)

14

8. Using a utility knife, carefully cut about an inch along the line that divides the curved part coming down from the neck of the bottle and the straight sides—make the cut just long enough so that scissors can be inserted.

9. Use the scissors to cut the rest of the way around the bottle, removing the top.

10. Cut the back out of the bottle, leaving the panel where the figure has been painted and the base. Cut two straight lines on either side of the figure, down to where the sides of the bottle begin to curve into the base. Cut along the line between the sides and the base and remove the back.

WARNING: Utility knives and scissors should never be used without adult supervision!

11. Weigh down the figure by mixing and pouring about one inch of plaster of Paris into the base. Carefully set your figure aside so that the plaster can set.

12. Add a tea-light candle (the type with a metal, not plastic, cup) in the center of the plaster of Paris base of each figure.

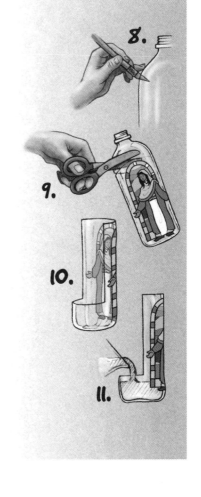

Light the candles and use your Nativity for worship.

This activity is for preteens, youth, and/or adults. If you have older children, they may wish to make the Nativity background on page 22 .

Note: If you have very young children, make photocopies of the Joy stained-glass window pattern on page 23 and let them color the stained-glass window. For younger elementary children, make photocopies of the Joy stained-glass window pattern and follow the directions to achieve the "stained-glass" appearance.

1 - Yellow

2 - Gold

3 - Orange

4 - Light Brown

5- Dark Brown

6 - Red

7 - Pink

8 - Purple

9 - Light Blue

10 - Deep Blue

11 - Light Green

12 - Deep Green

1 - Yellow
2 - Gold
3 - Orange
4 - Light Brown
5- Dark Brown
6 - Red
7 - Pink
8 - Purple
9 - Light Blue
10 - Deep Blue
11 - Light Green
12 - Deep Green

1 - Yellow

2 - Gold

3 - Orange

4 - Light Brown

5- Dark Brown

6 - Red

7 - Pink

8 - Purple

9 - Light Blue

10 - Deep Blue

11 - Light Green

12 - Deep Green

Seasons of Faith

1 - Yellow
2 - Gold
3 - Orange
4 - Light Brown
5- Dark Brown
6 - Red
7 - Pink
8 - Purple
9 - Light Blue
10 - Deep Blue
11 - Light Green
12 - Deep Green

Seasons of Faith

1 - Yellow
2 - Gold
3 - Orange
4 - Light Brown
5- Dark Brown
6 - Red
7 - Pink
8 - Purple
9 - Light Blue
10 - Deep Blue
11 - Light Green
12 - Deep Green

Activity: Nativity Background

The stable in which Jesus was born was probably a cave. Create your own stone, cave-like backdrop for the stained-glass Nativity.

You will need:
>   foam board
>   scraps of fabric in shades of brown and gray
>   wooden craft stick
>   white glue
>   scissors

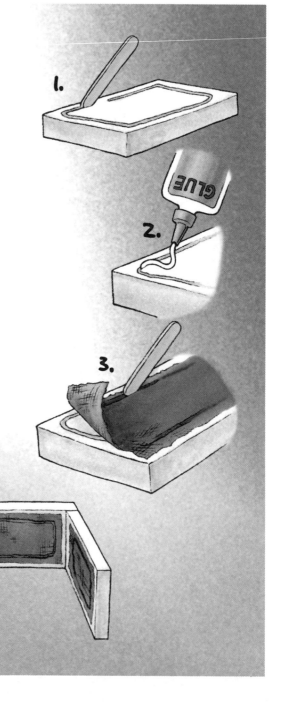

1. Use your wooden craft stick to score the outline of a stone into the foam board.

2. Spread white glue over the "stone" (foam board) and into the indentation created by the craft stick.

3. Lay a fabric scrap, a little larger than the "stone," on the glued portion. Then use the craft stick to press the edges down into the indentation.

    Repeat this step with two more pieces of foam board.

4. Place the pieces of foam board so that one forms the back of the cave and the other two form the sides of the cave.

5. Set up your cave behind your stained-glass Nativity.

Do you want another option to make a cave for your Nativity? Get a large piece of cardboard and paint stones on it.

Activity: Joy Stained-Glass Window

You will need:
crayons
dish or bowl
cotton balls
baby oil or vegetable oil

photocopies of stained-glass window picture
old newspapers
paper punch
yarn

Color the picture of the stained-glass window. Dip a cotton ball in a dish of baby oil or vegetable oil and spread it lightly over the back of the paper. Lay the picture on old newspaper to dry.

To hang it in a window, punch a hole in the top center of the picture and place yarn through the hole.

Seasons of Faith

Activity: Advent/Christmas Worship

To set the tone for the Advent season, a weekly worship as part of any group activity and/or in the home is the perfect thing. On pages 25-30 there is an Advent & Christmas Worship Booklet that may be photocopied and used in the local church setting or handed out to families to use at home.

Make a double-sided photocopy of the booklet. (If your copy machine doesn't have this feature, take it to a professional shop. For a small fee, they can do this quickly.) Stack the pages inside of each other—page 25 is the front and back cover. Fold the stack of papers in half, staple, and you will have a booklet. The layout below shows you the order to use to stack the papers for photocopying.

If you wish to use ONLY the ADVENT portion of the worship booklet, photocopy those sheets designated below with an "X," cut and paste them into the correct order, photocopy your "dummy" of the booklets, and then put it together. Be careful of the order of the pages so that the weeks come out in correct order.

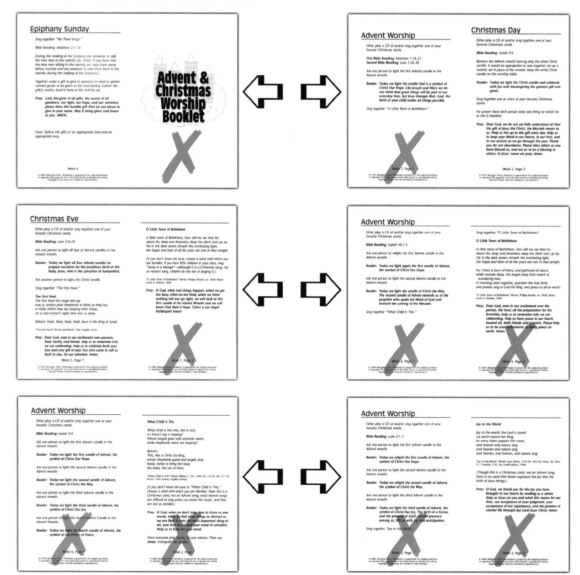

Epiphany Sunday

Sing together "We Three Kings."

Bible Reading: *Matthew 2:1-16*

During the reading of the Scripture, ask someone to add the wise men to the Nativity. (Note: If you have had the wise men sitting in the Nativity, take them away before worship and ask someone to add them back to the Nativity during the reading of the Scripture.)

Together make a gift to give to someone in need or gather canned goods to be given to a food pantry. Gather the gift(s) and/or food in front of the Nativity.

Pray: *God, the giver of all gifts, the source of all goodness, our light, our hope, and our salvation, please bless this humble gift that we are about to give in your name. May it bring glory and honor to you. Amen.*

Note: Deliver the gifts in an appropriate time and an appropriate way.

Advent & Christmas Worship Booklet

Christmas Day

Play a CD of and/or sing together one of your favorite Christmas carols.

Bible Reading: Isaiah 9:6

Remove the Advent wreath, leaving only the white Christ candle. It would now be appropriate to together set up a Nativity in place of the wreath. Keep the white Christ candle on the worship table.

Reader: **Today we light the Christ candle and celebrate with joy and thanksgiving the greatest gift ever given.**

Sing together one or more of your favorite Christmas carols.

For prayer have each person state one thing for which he or she is thankful.

Pray: **Dear God, we do not yet fully understand all that the gift of Jesus the Christ, the Messiah, means to us. Help us live up to this gift every day. Help us to keep your Word in our hearts, in our lives, and in our actions as we go through the year. Thank you for our abundance. Please bless others as you have blessed us, and use us to be a blessing to others. In Jesus' name we pray. Amen.**

Week 5, Page 2

Advent Worship

Play a CD of and/or sing together one of your favorite Christmas carols.

First Bible Reading: Matthew 1:18-25
Second Bible Reading: Luke 1:26-38

Ask one person to light the first Advent candle in the Advent wreath.

Reader: **Today we light the candle that is a symbol of Christ Our Hope. Like Joseph and Mary we do not think that great things will be part of our everyday lives, but Jesus changes that. God, the birth of your child makes all things possible.**

Sing together "O Little Town of Bethlehem."

Week 1, Page 1

Christmas Eve

Play a CD of and/or sing together one of your favorite Christmas carols.

Bible Reading: Luke 2:8-20

Ask one person to light all four Advent candles in the Advent wreath.

Reader: *Today we light all four Advent candles to prepare ourselves for the wondrous birth of this baby, Jesus, who is the salvation of humankind.*

Ask another person to light the Christ candle.

Sing together "The First Noel."

The First Noel

The first Noel the angel did say
was to certain poor shepherds in fields as they lay;
in fields where they lay keeping their sheep,
on a cold winter's night that was so deep.
Refrain: Noel, Noel, Noel, Noel, born is the King of Israel.

"The First Noel" Words and Music: Trad. English Carol.

Pray: *Dear God, even in our excitement over presents, food, family, and friends, help us to remember why we are celebrating. Help us to celebrate both your love and your gift of your Son who came to call us back to you for our salvation. Amen.*

Week 5, Page 1

O Little Town of Bethlehem

O little town of Bethlehem, how still we see thee lie;
above thy deep and dreamless sleep the silent stars go by.
Yet in thy dark streets shineth the everlasting light;
the hopes and fears of all the years are met in thee tonight.

(If you don't know the tune, choose a carol with which you are familiar. If you have little children, sing "Away in a Manger"—children do not tire of singing it.)

"O Little Town of Bethlehem" Words: Phillips Brooks, ca. 1868; Music: Lewis H. Redner, 1868.

Pray: *O God, when bad things happen, when we get too busy, when we are tired, when we think nothing will ever go right, we will look at this first candle of the Advent wreath and we will know that there is hope. Christ is our hope! Hallelujah! Amen!*

Week 1, Page 2

Advent Worship

Play a CD of and/or sing together one of your favorite Christmas carols.

Bible Reading: *Isaiah 40:1-5*

Ask one person to light the first Advent candle in the Advent wreath.

Reader: Today we light again the first candle of Advent, the symbol of Christ Our Hope.

Ask one person to light the second Advent candle in the Advent wreath.

Reader: Today we light the candle of Christ the Way. The second candle of Advent reminds us of the prophets who spoke the Word of God and foretold the coming of the Messiah.

Sing together "What Child Is This."

Sing together "O Little Town of Bethlehem"

O Little Town of Bethlehem

*O little town of Bethlehem, how still we see thee lie;
above thy deep and dreamless sleep the silent stars go by.
Yet in thy dark streets shineth the everlasting light;
the hopes and fears of all the years are met in thee tonight.*

*For Christ is born of Mary, and gathered all above,
while mortals sleep, the angels keep their watch of wondering love.
O morning stars together, proclaim the holy birth,
and praises sing to God the King, and peace to all on earth!*

"O Little Town of Bethlehem" Words: Phillips Brooks, ca. 1868; Music: Lewis H. Redner, 1868.

Pray: Dear God, even in our excitement over the parties, the food, and all the preparation for the festivities, help us to remember why we are celebrating. Help us have peace in our hearts toward all, both friends and enemies. Please help us to be your instruments to bring peace on earth. Amen.

Advent Worship

Play a CD of and/or sing together one of your favorite Christmas carols.

Bible Reading: Isaiah 9:6

Ask one person to light the first Advent candle in the Advent wreath.

Reader: *Today we light the first candle of Advent, the symbol of Christ Our Hope.*

Ask one person to light the second Advent candle in the Advent wreath.

Reader: *Today we light the second candle of Advent, the symbol of Christ the Way.*

Ask one person to light the third Advent candle in the Advent wreath.

Reader: *Today we light the third candle of Advent, the symbol of Christ Our Joy.*

Ask one person to light the fourth Advent candle in the Advent wreath.

Reader: *Today we light the fourth candle of Advent, the symbol of the Prince of Peace.*

What Child Is This

What child is this who, laid to rest,
on Mary's lap is sleeping?
Whom angels greet with anthems sweet,
while shepherds watch are keeping?

Refrain:
This, this is Christ the King,
whom shepherds guard and angels sing;
haste, haste to bring him laud,
the babe, the son of Mary.

"What Child Is This" Words: William C. Dix, 1865 (Lk. 2:6-20; Mt. 2:1-12); Music: 16th century English melody.

(If you don't know the tune to "What Child Is This," choose a carol with which you are familiar. Note this is a Christmas carol, not an Advent song; most Advent songs are difficult to sing unless you know the music, and they are not as familiar.)

Pray: O God, when we don't take time to listen to your Word, when we find other things to distract us, we are likely to miss the most important thing of all, your love for us, and your Word of salvation. Help us to listen for your Word.

Have everyone pray silently for one minute. Then say **Amen.** Extinguish the candles.

Advent Worship

Play a CD of and/or sing together one of your favorite Christmas carols.

Bible Reading: Luke 2:1-7

Ask one person to light the first Advent candle in the Advent wreath.

Reader: Today we light the first candle of Advent, the symbol of Christ Our Hope.

Ask one person to light the second Advent candle in the Advent wreath.

Reader: Today we light the second candle of Advent, the symbol of Christ the Way.

Ask one person to light the third Advent candle in the Advent wreath.

Reader: Today we light the third candle of Advent, the symbol of Christ Our Joy. The birth of a Savior, and the promise of God's eternal presence among us, fills us with joy and anticipation.

Sing together "Joy to the World."

Joy to the World

Joy to the world, the Lord is come!
Let earth receive her King;
let every heart prepare him room,
and heaven and nature sing,
and heaven and nature sing,
and heaven, and heaven, and nature sing.

"Joy to the World" Words: Isaac Watts, 1719 (Ps. 98:4-9); Music: Arr. from G. F. Handel, 1741, by Lowell Mason, 1848.

(Though this is a Christmas carol, not an Advent song, there is no carol that better expresses the joy that the birth of Jesus brings.)

Pray: O God, we thank you for the joy you have brought to our hearts by sending us a Savior. Help us focus on you and what this means for our lives, our acceptance of your judgment, your acceptance of our repentance, and the promise of eternal life through our Lord Jesus Christ. Amen.

Activity: Share Nativity Sets

Many people lovingly display their Nativity set each year. It not only adds meaning to the Christmas season, but it also usually has some fond memories attached. Others collect Nativity sets. One man I know has Nativity sets from around the world.

Give people an opportunity to share their Nativity sets with others. Below are three options for doing this. You will need a special place set up to display the Nativity sets where everyone can see them. (Option 3 is to be used in an individual classroom.)

Option 1: Pick a date on one of the Sundays of Advent for everyone who is interested to bring their family's most treasured Nativity to share with the congregation. Announce all the details in your newsletter, on your web site, or in the worship service—whatever methods you use to communicate.

Set up one or more tables in a very prominent place in the church. Drape the table with a beautiful cloth. Have "tent" place cards available along with markers so that each family can write their name on the place card and place it along with their Nativity set.

Serve refreshments and give everyone an opportunity to look at the variety of Nativity sets. Encourage people to talk about their Nativity sets.

Option 2: The same procedure as above only solicit Nativity sets that come from different cultures. You might want to personally contact people in your congregation that you know have Nativity sets from other cultures, and/or you may want to contact persons in your community from different ethnic backgrounds to join you for your chosen Sunday and bring their Nativity sets. Proceed as in option 1.

Option 3: Make a list for your class of the pieces of a Nativity: stable, Mary, Joseph, baby Jesus, wise men, shepherds, sheep, camel. Let each person sign up to bring ONE piece from his or her Nativity set. Then on the appointed day let each person put his or her Nativity piece on the worship table and see how your Nativity set takes shape. Probably the Nativity pieces will be of different sizes, shapes, colors, and materials. That's the joy of this activity.

You do not have to talk about this activity. The visual of the uniqueness of each piece put together to make a complete and pleasing scene will in itself demonstrate the complexity of God's world and the different viewpoints brought to the Christmas season.

Activity: Create a Gameboard

For a fun way to involve participants in a game, have the participants create a gameboard. The one described here is for Advent/Christmas. Take two or three sessions to create the gameboard. During the last couple of sessions, play the game as a review.

You will need:
Bibles	tape
scissors	brightly colored paper
markers	index cards
large sheets of newsprint or pieces of posterboard	

The "board" can be large sheets of newsprint or pieces of posterboard taped together. Have participants cut rectangles (1" by 2") from brightly colored paper. You may use the gameboard design on page 33 as an example. You could follow this gameboard exactly; or if you have some creative designers among you, come up with your own gameboard design. (Just remember the game must be "winnable," so take that into account when designing the gameboard.)

Lay out the gameboard by experimentally placing the colored squares where you think they should go. When the gameboard path has been designed to everyone's satisfaction, glue the rectangles into place.

Along the beginning section of the path, have someone write, "Mary hears the news." A little father along have someone write, "Joseph has a dream." Even farther along have someone write, "Mary and Joseph travel to Bethlehem." Then even farther along, "The shepherds hear the news." (If you decide you are going to take your study through Epiphany, add "The magi arrive.")

Have students cut out stars to place on every fifth square. They can be small and you can put them beside the words you have written on the squares, or you can make them larger and lay them down whether they fall on words or not. (The words are a reminder of the flow of the story.)

Invite participants to write reasons to move ahead, wait, or drop back on about every third or fourth empty gameboard space. Some suggestions: "Angel said, move ahead three spaces" or "Your donkey refuses to move, wait one turn" or "Move back two spaces while a Roman soldier passes by."

Divide participants into groups. Give each group fifteen index cards cut in half. Have each group write out questions from the Christmas Scriptures you will be studying. (They can add cards each week if you are spreading this activity across several weeks.) Have them work together as one group to weed out duplicate questions. To avoid duplicate questions, you could give each group a different Scripture.

Have the participants decide on the game rules as a group. Decide who goes first and how they will determine how many spaces to move. Decide whether it will be group answers or individual answers.

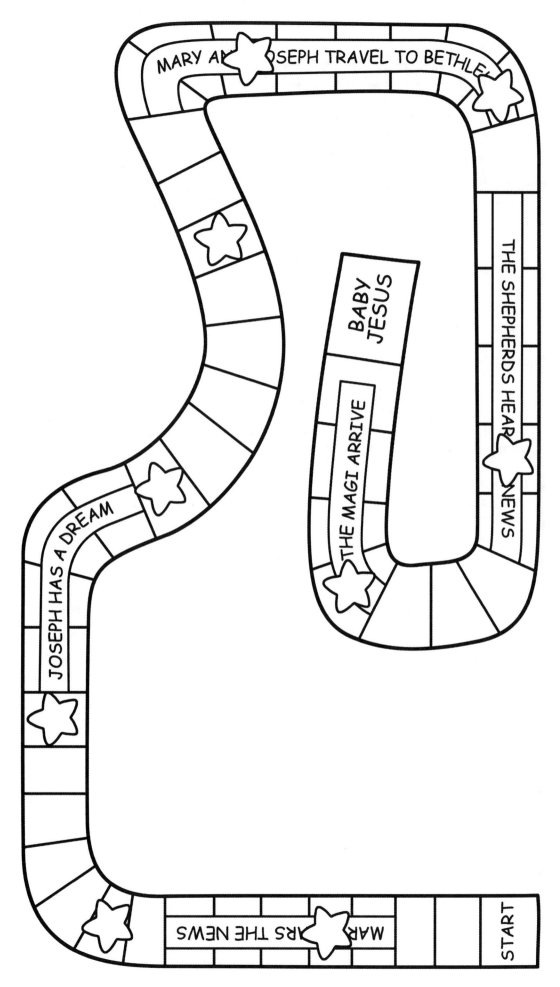

MARY AND JOSEPH TRAVEL TO BETHLEHEM

THE SHEPHERDS HEAR NEWS

BABY JESUS

THE MAGI ARRIVE

JOSEPH HAS A DREAM

MARY HEARS THE NEWS

START

Christmas

Jesus most probably was not born on December 25. In fact, we really do not know on what day he was born.

Why was December 25 chosen as Christmas Day? The story goes that December 25 was a day of a great pagan festival. The gaiety of the celebrations of the winter solstice—they thought of it as the "rebirth of the sun"—often drew Christians to join in the festivities.

Early Christians felt that celebrating the birth of the true "Son," the Light of the World, could not take place on a better day. It would center Christians on the true meaning of Christ and away from the pagan rituals that could draw them away from Christ. And so the celebration of the birth of the Savior, the Son of God, was created. All Christian churches today, with the exception of the Armenian church, celebrate Christmas—"Christ's Mass"— on December 25. The Armenian church celebrates the birth of Christ on January 6, the day of Epiphany. See page 54 for more on Epiphany.

Christmas has a strong basis in history and theology. It has been celebrated from very early times and has been used to celebrate God Incarnate—God with us. It is a time to focus on Jesus, the Messiah, the Savior, the Judge, the Redeemer, the one who calls us back to a relationship with God.

Early Christians struggled as we do between the secular parties and festivities and the spiritual aspects of celebrating the Incarnate God. It mirrors our daily struggle between the secular attractions of our everyday lives and the spiritual depth needed for a relationship with God.

Scriptures that are concentrated on for the celebration of Christmas are Isaiah 9:6-7 and Luke 2:8-20.

For prophetic scriptures that relate to Christmas, see the Prophecy Comparison Chart on page 13.

Christmas Around the World

Christmas is not just an American phenomenon; it is a worldwide celebration. Most Christmas traditions do not come from the Bible, but from symbolic events that have developed over time.

Truly Christian Christmas celebrations around the world do, however, have one thing in common: They are all customs that have their basis in the desire to celebrate God Incarnate in the baby Jesus. Many of the traditions also celebrate the act of giving from the biblical tradition of the wise men's gifts.

This year take time to emphasize the worldwide unity of the Advent/Christmas season. Try doing a "Christmas Around the World" time of teaching love and mutual respect for all Christians everywhere, whatever their customs may be.

Begin with the information on page 36.

Search the listed Internet sites. Remember, web site addresses can change and sites can close down. The listed Internet sites are only a starting point. Also, remember that not all information obtained on the Internet is accurate. Be discriminating—visit more than one site for confirmation. Gather games, crafts, recipes, and information to add to what is provided in this book.

The "Christmas Around the World" celebration information in this book is provided by continents. There will be many differences among individual countries on each continent. If you want to know more about any country, visit your local library or one of the Internet sites indicated.

Africa

Many people in the United States speak of Africa as if it is one large country. Africa is not a country; it is a continent. Its different countries have the unique foods, languages, and cultures that the different countries on any continent have.

Ethiopia (meaning "new flower") celebrates Christmas on January 7 after a day of fasting. After finishing the fast the people put on white clothes and go to church, where each person is given a candle. Once the candles are lit they walk around the church three times.

Cameroon is a country in Western Africa. It has a population of over 15,000,000 people. In Cameroon approximately forty percent of the people are Christians, forty percent practice African religion, and twenty percent are Muslims.

In Egypt, Christmas Day is a time for visiting friends and relatives. The people eat a dessert called Kahk—a flat, round cake filled with honey and dipped with powdered sugar.

African Christmas Greetings

Ethiopia: Melkm Ganna

Uganda: Osusuku Omusa

Sudan: Amuno no Natali

Nigeria: Barka da Kirsimati

Internet Site

www.santas.net/africanchristmas.htm

Activity: Shake Your Own Shekere

Shekeres (SHAY-ker-rays) are African percussion instruments that are used by world music performers all over the world. They are made from a calabash gourd, which is hollowed out, painted, and covered with a net decorated with shells or colorful beads. A player will shake the gourd so that the beads strike the sides of the gourd.

You probably don't have gourds available, so make a shekere out of a heavy plastic jug.

You will need:
    acrylic paint and paintbrushes
    clean, heavy plastic jug (like those that hold vinegar or bleach)
    yarn and ribbon
    beads

1. Using acrylic paint, paint a clean, heavy plastic jug.

2. Cut two pieces of yarn, one about 60 inches long and the other about 12 inches long.

3. String eight beads onto the 12-inch piece and tie the ends to form a beaded ring. Trim the ends.

4. Double up the 60-inch piece of yarn and wrap it around the jug just below the handle. Tie a triple knot, leaving the excess yarn hanging.

5. Cut four 26-inch pieces of yarn for the bead strands. Take one piece of yarn and tie a double knot about 4½ inches from the end. Place a bead on the yarn and push it down to the knot. Tie another double knot ¼ inch from the first bead, and add another bead. Continue adding beads until you have about eight beads on each strand.

6. Tie each strand, evenly spaced, to the doubled strand that is on the jug.

7. Place the jug on its side. Holding the beaded ring centered against the jug's bottom, tie each of the four strands to it. Leave a little slack in the strands so that they will shake against the jug.

8. Decorate the shekere by stringing beads on the loose ends of the excess yarn on the 60-inch strand. Tie ribbons around the neck of the jug.

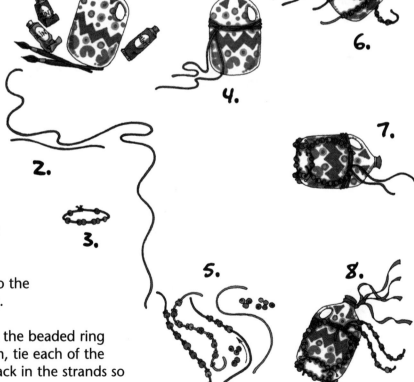
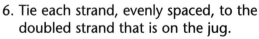

Asia

Asia is a continent of truly varied cultures. Christianity is not a large part of many Asian cultures, but it does flourish in some places.

Russia is the only country in two continents—Europe and Asia.

South Korea has a growing Christian population. Korean Christian churches are becoming very popular in the United States as well. In South Korea on Christmas Eve the youth of the churches have a traditional Christmas pageant. Then from midnight until early morning on Christmas morning they go caroling to the homes of church members. After a little sleep they go to Christmas morning worship service. Then there is a time of baptism and reception of new members into the church.

The Philippines is the only Asian country that is predominantly Christian. Here the Christmas celebration starts nine days before Christmas at a mass where the story of the birth of Jesus is read from the Bible.

Asian Christmas Greetings
Russia: Pozdrevlyayu s prazdnikom Rozhdestva is Novim Godom

China: Singdaan faailok

Hong Kong: Ching Chi Shentan

Philippines: Bikol maog-ganm Pasko

Korea: Sung Tan Chuk Ha

Japan: Kurisumasu omedeto

Internet Site
www.santas.net/aroundtheworld.htm

Seasons of Faith

Activity: Listen to Me

Play with your group the Vietnamese game called "Listen to Me." In this game one participant is "It." Blindfold the person who is "It" and have everyone stand in a circle around him or her.

Say: "It" will stand still while I count to ten. While I am counting, all the other players quietly scatter. When I stop counting, you must freeze and begin clapping. "It" will try to find you and touch you. Once you have been touched, you are out of the game. When "It" has touched all of the players, we will start again with a new "It."

Play the game. If you have a large group you may wish to have two players be "It."

Activity: Tin Can Hide and Seek

In the Philippines the children play a game that is a variation on Hide and Seek. Everyone stands at a designated starting place. The person who is "It" throws an empty tin can as far as possible. When the can is thrown everybody scatters to hide. "It" runs and picks up the can and returns to the starting place. Once "It" arrives at the starting place, "It" gets to begin seeking those who are hiding.

Australia

Australia gets many of its customs from England and other places. Many of the things they do in Australia would not be foreign to us. However, Christmas comes in the summer in Australia. (It is still on December 25, but that is summertime in Australia.)

Imagine picnics on the beach and Christmas caroling in the park late at night in your shorts. These are some of the characteristics of an Australian Christmas.

Australia even has a Christmas Island! There are two Christmas Islands: one is in the Pacific Ocean in Micronesia, and the other is in the Indian Ocean and is administered by Australia. It is called Christmas Island because December 25 is the date that Captain William Mynors "discovered" the island. Ironically, though it is named Christmas Island, less than twenty percent of the population is Christian.

Internet Sites
www.cvc.org/christmas/australia.htm
www.shoal.net.au/~seabreeze/christmas.html

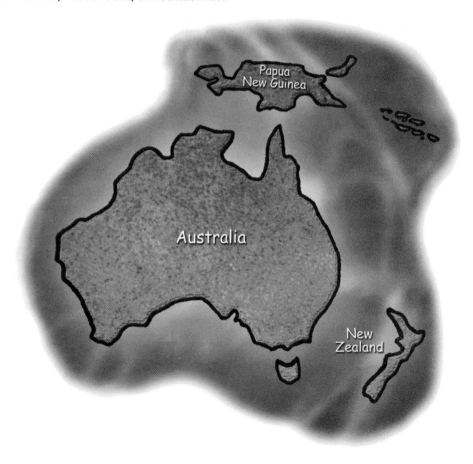

Activity: Barbecue

If you want to celebrate Christmas in the Australian manner, plan a barbecue. In Australia barbecue does not mean a particular type of food dripping with sauce; it means food cooked outside over a grill.

Since it may be rather cold in your area at Christmas, substitute an electric grill and have the barbecue inside. You might even want to make it a beach party, since many Australians spend Christmas on the beach. Just decorate the room in a beach theme with lawn chairs, beach towels, a sun umbrella, and beach toys.

Eat picnic style.

Close your party by dimming the lights, lighting candles, and singing traditional Christmas carols. We go Christmas caroling in the United States as well, but in most areas, not in our shorts. To keep the feeling that it's warm, you may need to do your caroling inside.

Europe

Europe is a continent of varied cultures, most of which have a rich tradition in Christianity. Just like many people immigrate to the United States, many people from many places and many religious backgrounds are immigrating to Europe.

As previously noted, Russia is the only country in two continents; it is in both Europe and Asia.

It is said that the use of the Christmas tree comes from Germany. Also, the use of holly comes from a German legend associating holly with the crown of thorns placed on Jesus' head at the crucifixion.

The tradition of burning a yule log seems to have come from the Scandinavian countries of Norway and Denmark.

European Christmas Greetings
Spain: Felices Navidad

Italy: Buon Natale

Norway: God jul

Poland: Wesolych Swiat

Romania: Sarbatori Fericite

Germany: Frohliche Weihnachten

France: Joyeux Noel

Greece: Kala Christougena

Austria: Frohe Weihnacten

Ireland: Nollaig Shona Dhuit
        or Nodlaig mhaith chugnat

England: Happy Christmas

Internet Sites
www.polishworld.com/christmas
www.german-way.com/german/christmas.html

Activity: Christmas Party Crackers

A really fun Christmas tradition from England is the Christmas party cracker. This is a gaily wrapped party favor. There is always a surprise inside of the cracker.

You will need:
>Christmas wrapping paper
>paper towel tubes
>string or ribbon
>small favors to put inside of the crackers
>scissors

1. Decide how many crackers you want to make. Cut your paper towel tubes into the desired number of equal lengths.

2. Fill each length of paper towel tube with the small favor(s).

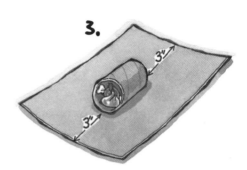

3. Roll each tube in a piece of Christmas wrapping paper large enough to lap over each end by at least 3 inches.

4. Do not tape the paper; instead twist the ends of the paper and seal your cracker by tying it with bright string or ribbon.

To make this more meaningful, why not put a small piece of paper with a verse from the Christmas story into the cracker along with the surprise?

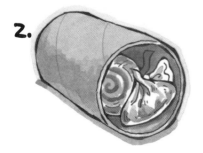

South and Central America

Most of the countries in South and Central America share a strong Roman Catholic influence.

In many South and Central American countries, one of the oldest traditional Christmas season celebrations is Las Posadas. It is a celebration that was actually created by Father Diego de Soria in the late 1500s to introduce Christianity to the New World. The celebration is a reenactment of Mary and Joseph searching for a place to stay in Bethlehem. Many churches in the United States today celebrate Las Posadas with a full service or a smaller, modified version of the celebration. Check with your pastor or Christian educator to see if your church has information on this great celebration.

Latin American Christmas Greetings
Brazil: Feliz Natal
Peru: Yomporcha' ya' nataya
Columbia: Mamak wejejeraka
Aruba: Bon Pasko
Bolivia: Sooma Nawira-ra

Internet Sites
www.santas.net/aroundtheworld.htm

Activity: South American Fiesta

Decorations

Deck the halls with lots of brightly colored paper flowers. You can sometimes buy these in stores or you can make them using chenille sticks and colored tissue paper. Craft books have several different versions. You might want to put strings of colored paper flowers on your Christmas tree. Several South American countries do this.

Prominently display a Nativity set—especially the manger. This is always a big part of a South American Christmas. Place bright red poinsettias around the room. This is a very popular Christmas flower in South America—it represents an old Aztec tradition representing the blood of sacrifice. This has been adopted by and changed by Christians over the centuries to represent the blood of Christ. It evolved into a Christian Christmas symbol because Christmas is the time of year that poinsettias grow.

Dress

December is summer in South America, so bring out the summer clothes—preferably in bright colors—for the fiesta. Remember that South America is known for colorful clothing (as is summer), and that this is a celebration. Color is always appropriate.

Music

Play Spanish music. You may be able to find a recording of "Feliz Navidad." With so many Hispanic persons in the United States, you may be able to find other Christmas music recorded in Spanish in your local music stores. Or perhaps you are lucky enough to have someone in your church or community who can play and or sing songs in Spanish, and maybe you can have them teach some Christmas carols in Spanish. Look in your hymnal; many hymnals now contain some hymns with Spanish text. Don't forget—Brazil is also in South America, and its language is not Spanish, but Brazilian Portuguese. Wouldn't it be great to find some Christmas music in Portuguese! Portuguese may be harder to find, but if you live in a large city, you might be able to do so. The Internet might also be a valuable tool in your search.

Food

Research the cuisine of various South American countries on the Internet. You should easily be able to find recipes from any country in which you are interested. Assign different people to research different countries and have each one bring a dish from that country.

Worship

Make a Las Posadas procession a prelude to worship. Some of the worship resources of different denominations have a Las Posadas celebration. Ask your pastor. If your denomination does not have an outline for this service, call a local Hispanic church (many areas have them); they should be able to help you.

North America

The United States has an English, French, Spanish, and Native cultural background, as well as people and cultural influences from most of the world. This makes for some interesting traditions, but we are often so used to them that we do not recognize them as unique anymore.

Canada has both an English and a French heritage as well as having many Native cultures.

Mexico has many of the traditions of Central and South America.

One Christmas link between Canada and the United States is not very well known. In 1917 two ships ran into each other in the Halifax harbor. The explosion caused great damage to the city and killed and injured many people. The city of Boston, Massachusetts, sent food and supplies to help the city. Doctors also made the trip to Halifax to help treat the injured. The city of Halifax was very thankful for the help from Boston. Ever since Halifax sends a Christmas tree to Boston every year to commemorate the special relationship between the two cities.

In the United States we put up Christmas trees (which are thought to come from Germany), we eat foods from many different countries (depending upon your own background), we sing Christmas carols (many of which came from different parts of Europe), and we put out Nativity sets. Many churches even have live nativities (a tradition which began with St. Francis of Assisi).

North American Christmas Greetings

United States: Merry Christmas

Mexico: Feliz Navidad

Inupiaq Tribe (Alaska):
   Annaurri Aniruq

French Canadian:
   Joyeux Noel

Internet Site
www.mexconnect.com/mex_/feature/xmasindex.html

Activity: Papel Picado

It would be great fun to "deck the halls" (and doorways) with papel picado. Papel picado means "pierced paper," and these banners can be seen throughout Mexico. This art is not exclusive to Mexico; it has been found in other cultures as well.

In Mexico these colorful banners are used as an inexpensive way to decorate for every festive occasion. Different colors are used for different holidays. For Easter purple would be the preferred color; for Christmas rainbow colors may be used.

You will need:
    tissue paper in various colors (traditional size is 15 x 10 inches, but use any size that works)
    small sharp scissors
    string
    glue stick or stapler and staples

1. Fold the paper in half so that you have a rectangle. Fold this paper in half two more times.

2. Cut away shapes from both folded edges. Do NOT cut all the way across the rectangle or it will fall apart. Cut out more shapes in the center of the paper. (This is much like the way we make paper snowflakes in the United States.)

3. Unfold the paper partially to cut additional shapes.

4. Open your papel picado completely and hang it by gluing or stapling the flap over a length of string. You will need to glue several of these cutouts next to each other on the string.

5. Hang them around the walls, across the doorways, or anywhere you like to make your Christmas celebration colorful and beautiful.

Hint: For fun make each cutout a radically different design.

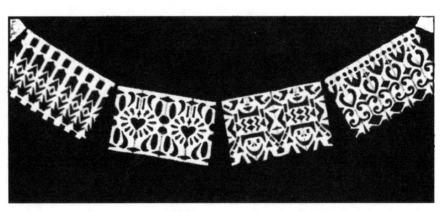

Variation: After folding the paper in half the first time, the second time fold the paper at an angle, just up to the flap. Then fold two more times and scallop the uneven edge.

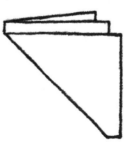

Activity: Christian Christmas Tree

Using Christian ornaments provides an opportunity to express and celebrate our Christian heritage. Most of us are familiar with the Chrismon Tree (Christ Monogram). Chrismons were developed by Mrs. Francis Spencer, who gave the copyright to Ascension Lutheran Church in Danville, Virginia. Chrismons are usually white and gold, the colors of the church season. (See Colors of the Christian Year chart, page 9).

While many people assume that any tree with predominately Christian ornaments is a Chrismon tree, there are many ways to decorate a Christian Christmas tree. Some of these ornaments predate the Chrismon tree (for example, the candy cane and angels), and some of them are newer and mass produced (for example, the butterfly, which represents new life, is becoming a popular Christmas ornament in all kinds of forms).

You can decorate a tree using only specifically Christmas ornaments, or your can add other Christian symbols, for example, the butterfly (new life), the empty cross (symbol of the resurrection of our Lord), the donkey (a symbol of Christmas and of Palm Sunday), and so forth. *You will need:*

artificial Christmas tree and stand	tree skirt
scissors	ornament hooks

craft items to make ornaments:
felt or cloth, fiberfill, needle and thread, yarn
or
foam board, glitter, glue, gold trim
or
paper, baby oil, crayons, cotton balls

Use the symbol patterns on pages 49-52 to make Christian symbols for a tree (meanings are listed below). Make an ornament out of felt or cloth and stuff it with fiberfill; cut a design out of foam board and decorate it with glue, gold trim, and glitter; or cut an ornament out of paper, color it, use baby oil to coat it, and make it into a type of "stained-glass" ornament. There are Easter patterns on pages 111 and 112 and Pentecost patterns on page 128. These could also be used in making Christian Christmas tree ornaments.

The Fish: One of the first Christian symbols, used to help Christians identify one another.

Rose Within a Star: The five-pointed star is an Epiphany symbol representing the visit of the wise men to the infant Messiah. The rose symbolizes both the Nativity and messianic prophecy.

Entwined Circles: Symbol of the Trinity—Father, Son, and Holy Spirit.

Greek Cross and X Monogram: A symbol for Christ—a Greek Cross superimposed on X (chi), the first letter of the Greek word for Christ.

Star: The star of Bethlehem.

Chi Rho With Alpha and Omega: A symbol for Jesus our Lord as the beginning and end.

Staff With Alpha and Omega: The staff is the symbol of Jesus, the Good Shepherd; the Alpha and Omega symbolize our Lord as the beginning and end.

Seasons of Faith

52

Activity: Global Christmas Service

We all do service projects for Christmas in our own communities, and we should continue to do so, but the Advent/Christmas season is also an important time to look at the Word of God in a global context.

Most Christian denominations have missionaries in some country around the world. If not, these days everyone knows of someone in an organization that helps people globally.

Why not take Christian outreach global? Contact your denomination for a list of missionaries. (If your church does not have a missionary it is sponsoring, contact an agency such as the Red Cross, Doctors Without Borders, UNICEF, Church World Service, or Heifer International.)

Discover what the needs are and then decide what need you want to take on and how you will fulfill it.

For example: One missionary in the Philippines would give food to her impoverished students, leaving herself short of food. A church group started sending small amounts of money from their service projects that she could use to feed herself or her students. They did this all year, adding a special big offering at Christmas.

Consider these possibilities for a Christmas service project:

• Heifer International sends out a catalog for Christmas—an interesting catalog. You can buy animals through this catalog—but not for yourself. The animals you purchase go to help families in different parts of the world start their own herds. This helps them eventually become self-sufficient.

• Many children of the world do not get adequate medical treatment. Why not raise money for one of the organizations that attempts to bring medicine to children? Sometimes you hear of specific children being brought to the United States for expensive treatments that cannot be handled in their own countries. A donation could be made to a fund for one of these children.

• Consider helping children from war-torn countries. Children do not start wars, but they are often the victims of wars. Adopt the children of a country devastated by war. Most churches have programs for helping children of other countries.

Special Note: *There are many other charitable organizations out there. Just be careful in your research and make sure that it is a legitimate organization. The Internet has opened up new opportunities for fraud to take place.*

Epiphany

The original celebration day of the Advent/Christmas/Epiphany season was Epiphany. This was a celebration of the revelation of God's light and power—Christ (John 1:1–2:11). This was the original day on which this revelation, Christ, was celebrated.

Today Eastern churches continue to emphasize Epiphany while Western churches emphasize Advent. For Western churches Christmas Day begins the twelve days of celebration of Christmas, and Epiphany is the twelfth day of that celebration—the celebration of the visit of the wise men to the Christ Child (Matthew 2:1-12). In the United States we put most of our emphasis on Advent and Christmas Day, while in many countries in Europe the emphasis is upon Christmas through Epiphany. In the Eastern Orthodox Church Epiphany is especially important.

Epiphany is immersed in the imagery of light:

• The light from the star that led the wise men from the East to Jesus. (The trip took approximately two years. The wise men did not visit Jesus when he was a baby, but when he was a toddler.)

• Jesus, the Light of the World.

This is often the day when the flight to Egypt is also dealt with because that event was set off by the visit of the wise men to Herod. Again this chain of events is tied to prophecies of the Messiah (see the Prophecy Comparison Chart on page 13).

Advent/Christmas/Epiphany—If we keep the meanings of these holidays before us they provide us with a firm theological understanding of Jesus, the Messiah, the Son of God. This season also provides us with the opportunities to begin to understand what is fully revealed to us through the rest of the Christian Year.

Activity: Star Melts

Everyone loves candy. As a way to symbolize the star leading the wise men to Jesus, make star melts. These candies can be enjoyed by the group or they can be a treat that is delivered to persons who are homeless, persons who are in nursing homes, or persons whose ability to leave home is limited. (Why not put them in bags or baskets decorated with stars?)

You will need:
   oven (a small toaster oven will work)
   baking sheets
   aluminum foil
   peppermint candies
   star-shaped cookie cutters
   spray cooking oil

1. Preheat the oven to 325 degrees.

2. Cover a baking sheet with aluminum foil.

3. Coat metal star-shaped cookie cutters with spray cooking oil.

4. Place several peppermint candies inside the cookie cutters on baking sheets covered with aluminum foil.

5. Bake 6 to 7 minutes.

6. Let the cookie cutters cool, then pop out your star melts.

Activity: Epiphany Bible Bookmark

You will need:
> yellow paper or felt
> scissors
> paper punch
> ribbon
> glue

1. Trace the star pattern on page 57 on yellow paper or yellow felt.

2. Cut out the star.

3. Punch holes about halfway down the points at the top and bottom of the star. (See the black dots on the pattern.)

4. Thread a piece of ribbon (about 10½ inches long) from the back of the star through the holes. Pull the ribbon tight, leaving some ribbon at both the top and bottom of the star.

5. Lightly glue the ribbon at the center on the back of the star to keep the ribbon from sliding.

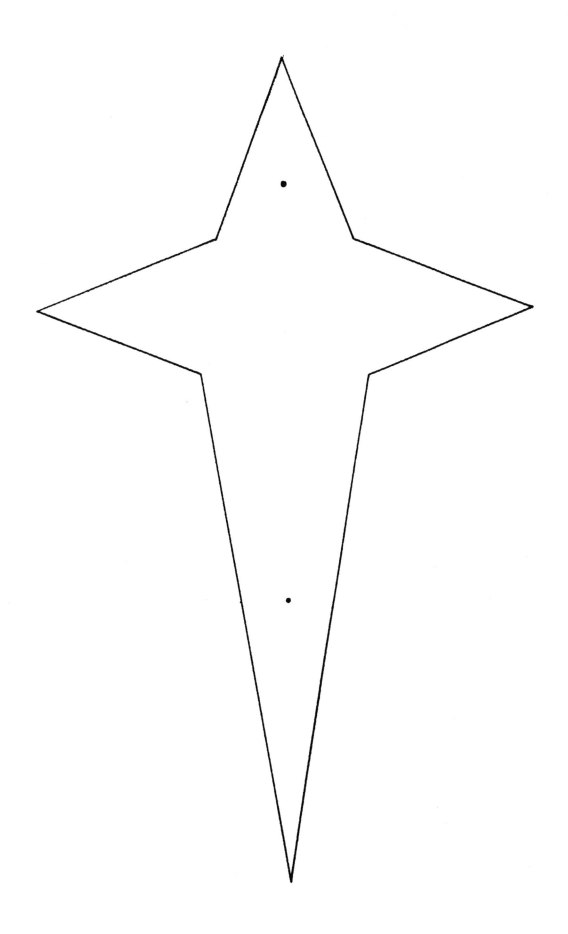

Seasons of Faith

Activity: Epiphany Service Project

In America we spend a lot of time with wonderful Christmas projects. Many European countries concentrate on Epiphany. Want to place a little more emphasis on Epiphany? Do an Epiphany Service Project.

Pick an organization that works with babies: a hospital, an orphanage, a battered women's shelter, a place that takes care of babies born with AIDS, or an agency in your community with which you are familiar.

Hold a baby shower for this organization. Involve the whole church. Discover the needs of the organization. Do they need diapers? food? baby clothing? toys? Whatever they need, go by their list. It is not helpful to give extras to an organization that really is hurting for the basics. (Or maybe the organization does have the basics, but no extras. You need to ask the organization before you start your project.)

Your baby shower could take the form of a "money tree." What non-profit organization doesn't need extra money?

Decorate plain paper bags or boxes with stars (you can do this with stamps and stamp pads or with sponges and paint). Make a large gift card with stars drawn or stamped on it. Let everyone involved in the project sign the card as they drop off their gifts.

On the day of Epiphany or the Monday after Epiphany Sunday, a designated group can deliver the gifts.

Caution: Most organizations can't handle large groups of visitors. However, some organizations may be able to give a tour to a larger group if arranged in advance. In any case, you do not wish to interfere with the daily operations of the agency you have chosen.

Note: Another option would be for your church to "adopt" a needy single mother with a young child and hold the shower for her. Things like food, diapers, a special outfit, and a special toy for the child would go a long way toward helping out a struggling single mom.

A Time Between:
Baptism of the Lord
Transfiguration Sunday
Shrove Tuesday

Baptism of the Lord

The Season After the Epiphany is the time between Epiphany and Ash Wednesday. It begins with the first Sunday after Epiphany, which celebrates the baptism of Jesus (Matthew 3:13-17; Mark 1:9-11; Luke 3:21-22; John 1:29-34).

The first Sunday after Epiphany Sunday in worship concentrates on the baptism of Jesus, and the following Sundays usually are thought of as a time to concentrate on the life and ministry of Jesus.

Transfiguration Sunday

The Season After the Epiphany ends with Transfiguration Sunday. This is the Sunday that celebrates when Jesus was transfigured before Peter, James, and John: "Suddenly a bright cloud overshadowed them, and from the cloud a voice said, 'This is my Son, the Beloved; with him I am well pleased'" (Matthew 17:5). This verse repeats the words heard at Jesus' baptism (Matthew 3:17).

The story of the Transfiguration is very difficult to understand, and it is seldom introduced to young children. However, even older children can begin to understand the significance of God revealing to the disciples that Jesus is the Son before the final story of Jesus' suffering, crucifixion, and resurrection.

Activity: Videotape Baptism Stories

You will need:
> video camera
> blank videocassette tape
> television and VCR to show tape

To discover what baptism means in the lives of people, videotape interviews with members of your congregation. You could do these interviews yourself and then show them to a group studying baptism, or you could have the participants do the interviews as part of the baptism study.

To get a wide range of baptism stories, try to discover who in your congregation might have different denominational backgrounds (many churches today are made up of people who come from other Christian denominations and often their baptism experiences are different). Also attempt to interview people of different ages—a newly baptized preteen, a youth, a younger adult, a middle adult, and an older adult.

Some possible questions to ask:

• How old were you when you were baptized?

• Do you remember your baptism?

• What do you remember about it? Describe your baptism.

• Who decided you would be baptized (yourself, parent, church tradition)?

• Why were you baptized?

• How were you baptized (sprinkling, pouring, immersion)?

• What does your baptism mean to you?

Activity: optical Illusions

The Transfiguration is a very important story, and it takes abstract thinking skills to understand it. However, you can help people begin to understand by working with optical illusions. After all, the Transfiguration of Jesus took the Jesus that the disciples knew and gave the disciples a completely new viewpoint of Jesus. Though Jesus was familiar to them they began to see him in a new way (Matthew 16:13-20; 17:1-8).

Optical Illusion Activities

Activity 1—In the library find a book that shows different optical illusions (young/old woman is one of the most famous examples, but there are many others). Show the illusions to your group and let them discover both ways to look at the illusion. Discuss how this might relate to how the disciples viewed Jesus.

Activity 2—Make a Two-Way Picture
You will need:

white drawing paper	construction paper
markers	scissors
pencils	glue
ruler	posterboard

These pictures can be done individually or the group can work together. On a 6- by 6-inch sheet of white drawing paper, use markers to illustrate the disciples and Jesus climbing the mountain. On another 6- by 6-inch sheet of drawing paper, have them draw a picture of the Transfiguration with Moses and Elijah.

Using a pencil, draw lines ½ inch apart on the back of a 6- by 12-inch piece of construction paper. The lines should each be 6 inches long. Fold the construction paper accordion-style along the lines. (It is helpful to score the lines before folding.) Glue the ends of the folded construction paper to a 6- by 9-inch piece of posterboard.

Mark lines ½ inch apart on the back of the pictures and cut the pictures into strips. Keep the strips in order. Glue the strips along the folds of the construction paper, alternating pieces of both pictures.

View the two-way picture by holding it at an angle so that you can see one picture, then turn it to see the other. This will help your participants understand that the disciples viewed Jesus one way when they walked up the mountain, and another way when they walked down the mountain after the Transfiguration.

Shrove Tuesday

Originally "shrove" meant to hear confessions—something people did before entering the holy season of Lent.

Shrove Tuesday is no longer a big day in most Protestant churches, but celebrating Shrove Tuesday can really help clarify the meaning of Ash Wednesday.

The day before Ash Wednesday was the last day before Lent. Lent was seen as a time of penance (confessing). It was a very solemn time, and Lent was taken very seriously. People did not have parties during Lent, and they refrained from eating rich foods such as butter, milk, and eggs—any of the items with fat that make eating such a pleasure.

People had to use up these items so that they wouldn't spoil during Lent. So it became a tradition to eat things such as pancakes. It has been said that people ate greater numbers of meals on Shrove Tuesday before the deprivation of Lent.

Gradually this type of eating gave way to partying and other forms of celebration. Slowly, because of the amount of rich foods consumed, this day became known as Fat Tuesday. Many celebrations today have become very elaborate and nonreligious in tone. Probably the most well known celebration before Lent is Mardi Gras (which is French for "Fat Tuesday").

A church, however, can have a very fun, fattening Shrove or Fat Tuesday and still incorporate the original meaning of the day (see page 64).

Activity: Pancake Supper

You will need:
   electric griddles
   pancake batter
   sausage, ham, and bacon
   plates, napkins, and utensils

A pancake supper is very traditional for Shrove Tuesday. Remember this was seen as a time for using up fat, so eat up.

Ask to borrow electric griddles ahead of time. Have every family who attends the supper bring one batch of pancake batter (their favorite recipe). To make this a true feast, cook up some sausage, ham, and bacon. Make sure everyone gets a lot to eat. That's the point.

A variation of this would be to have a pancake supper as a fundraiser with the money going to your favorite mission project.

Activity: Party Hearty

You will need:

streamers	plastic beads, coins, and trinkets
masks	paper bags (optional)
CDs and CD player	king's cake

Throw a Mardi Gras ("Fat Tuesday") party. Put up streamers, have people wear masks, provide lots of music, and have lots of inexpensive plastic beads, coins, and small trinkets to throw. Gather folks around at some point and throw the beads, coins, and trinkets. (You might have participants decorate paper bags before you do the throwing. They can use them to store what they catch.) Everyone—male and female—should wear their beads.

Have lots of food. If you have a bakery near you that can make a king's cake (a cake with a small plastic baby doll baked inside one of the pieces), you might want to have one for the party. (You can buy a very small plastic baby doll made to be baked in a king's cake, or you can substitute a bean.) The king's cake is said by some to represent the baby Jesus. Others say it is to represent the three kings (wise men who visited Jesus). The king's cake tradition began as an Epiphany tradition and now goes through Shrove Tuesday. The person who receives the piece of cake that contains the plastic baby doll is said to have good luck all year. (They are also according to tradition supposed to host the next party or bring the next king's cake, but since you will be doing this only one night, you can omit that part of the tradition.)

Play some active, rowdy games. Then close the party with a short worship service in which you remind everyone that Shrove Tuesday is a time to party before the time of quiet reflection and repentance of Lent, which begins with Ash Wednesday. Be sure to invite everyone to the next day's Ash Wednesday service.

The contrast between the party and the Ash Wednesday service makes for a stronger impression of what the Lenten season is about.

Ash Wednesday
Lent

Ash Wednesday

Ash Wednesday is a solemn, holy day. There are no parties and no special foods. Ash Wednesday marks the beginning of the Lenten season.

The uniqueness of Ash Wednesday is the worship service associated with the day and the fact that this day is the official beginning of the forty days of Lent.

Ash Wednesday is so named because of the ashes used to mark the foreheads of worshipers. The palm branches from the previous year's Palm Sunday service are burned in a prescribed manner and the ashes reserved for the next Ash Wednesday service.

The Ash Wednesday service is a service of public penance. Worshipers are called forward to the altar rail, and the minister applies the ashes with his or her thumb to form the sign of the cross on the forehead of each worshiper. This is a public declaration of the need for repentance.

This service is very old in the history of the church. In 1191 the Pope made it an official act of the church. At one point the Protestant reformers abandoned the practice of the ashes on the forehead. However, many of today's Protestant churches have begun again to practice this service in recognition of its importance in focusing the season of Lent upon repentance.

Activity: Attend Ash Wednesday Service

As a group attend your church's Ash Wednesday Service (especially if you had a Shrove Tuesday party). This will help your group understand the importance of preparing themselves for the Lenten season and give Lent a more prominent position in the life of the church. Before you attend the service you might ask the minister to explain to your group the meaning of the service and of the ashes being placed on the forehead of the worshipers.

Activity: Prepare the Heart

You will need:
　　index cards
　　pens or markers

Lent is a season that is about penitence and preparing the heart for the salvation that Easter morning brings to us.

The first time your group meets in Lent (or immediately before Lent) help group members prepare their hearts. Ask each participant to move his or her chair as far away from other people as possible. Darken the room somewhat. Ask for silence. You may keep the room silent or play soft music to set the mood. Give each participant two index cards and a pen or marker.

As preparation for group worship, **Say:**

• **Think about the things that you have done this year for which you need to ask forgiveness.**

• **Choose the two things of which you most need to repent and write them on your first index card. No one will see this card except for you.**

• **Think about something for which you need to forgive someone else. On your second index card write this down. No one will see this card except for you.**

Ask everyone to bring their chairs back together for worship. During the worship ask the participants to pray about what is on their two cards and to do so every day of Lent. They are to keep their cards where they will see them every day—in their pockets, in a purse, in their Bibles, on a bulletin board—wherever they will see the cards and be reminded to pray. They are to mark on their index cards each day (whatever mark will help them remember) when they have prayed about these things.

Let them know that you wish them to report back at the end of Lent whether or not they did this activity.

Lent

Originally Lent was the period before Easter when converts were instructed in the Christian religion. This instruction was to prepare them for baptism, which at that time took place on Easter.

The observance of the resurrection of Christ was three days—Friday through Sunday. A fast of forty hours was the normal preparation for Easter Sunday. At some period this was extended to several weeks before Easter and named Lent. Pope Gregory extended the Lenten season to forty days by adding four days, from Ash Wednesday to the first Sunday of Lent. This forty days was a parallel to Jesus' forty days of fasting in the wilderness. For the Western church Lent now begins with Ash Wednesday.

The forty days of Lent do NOT include Sundays, since all Sundays are considered to be small Easters in celebration of the Resurrection.

Since the forty days of Lent parallel the forty days of the fasting and temptation of Christ, it has become customary to use Lent as a time of preparation. Frivolity is put aside and people are to prepare themselves and use this as a time of penance.

Many people give up something for Lent as a reminder of the season. Others take on new spiritual disciplines such as prayers of repentance, spiritual journaling, and extra service to others.

Churches often use this as a time to study the life, teachings, and miracles of Jesus.

Lenten Study

This six-week Lenten study is based on the messiahship of Jesus Christ. It deals with who Jesus is—Jesus the acknowledged Son of God, who is tempted by Satan, teaches and heals, is persecuted by the existing religious authorities, and is arrested, tried, and crucified.

The six sessions of this Lenten study are:

> *Session 1: Jesus Is Baptized—Matthew 3:13-17*
>
> *Session 2: Jesus Is Tempted—Matthew 4:1-11*
>
> *Session 3: Jesus Heals—Matthew 8:1-17*
>
> *Session 4: Jesus' Triumphal Entry Into Jerusalem—Matthew 21:1-11*
>
> *Session 5: Jesus Cleansing the Temple to Jesus' Crucifixion—Matthew 21:12–27:66*
>
> *Session 6: Jesus Is Raised From the Dead—Matthew 28; Mark 16:1-8; Luke 24:1-12; John 20:1-10*

For the craft and game activities, divide participants into ongoing groups. The groups formed for the first session will be their group for any group-work for the next six weeks. If new participants come to the study, they may be added to the existing groups.

You may choose to do only one of the craft activities, or if you have a large group you may want to have some participants work on one activity while some participants work on a different one.

Note: *The six-week Lenten study is on pages 70-80. Detailed descriptions of the activities in this study are described on pages 81-105. These activities are listed separately because several are used over the entire six weeks, and any of these activities may stand alone or be adapted to use within other studies.*

Lenten Study – Week 1

Bible: Matthew 3:13-17—Jesus Is Baptized

- **Arrival Activity: Water Stations and Long Distance Pouring**
Use the activities on pages 81 and 82.

- **Opening Activity: Group-Building Game**
Use the activity on page 83. When beginning a six-week study, especially if you have participants who don't know each other well and/or are of different ages, a group-building activity is essential.

- **Bible Activity 1: Read the Bible Story**
Have someone who reads well dramatically read the Bible story, Matthew 3:13-17.

Explain to the participants that Jesus' baptism is not part of the Lenten story itself, but it is the first public acknowledgment of Jesus as the Son of God, the Messiah.

- **Bible Activity 2: Lenten Cross**
Have each group begin a Lenten Cross (page 84).

- **Game: Begin Preparing Floor Game**
This game will actually be played in sessions 4-6. It is described on pages 88 and 89.

- **Craft Activity 1: Begin Lenten Mural**
Use the activity on page 85.

- **Craft Activity 2: Begin Lenten Tree**
Use the activity on pages 102 and 103.

- **Service Activity: Begin a Lenten Service Project**
Research agencies that help people in your area or somewhere around the world. Bring the list to the group. Let the group add to the list. Then together narrow down the possibilities and choose a service project. Outline a plan about how you are to carry out the project. Working as a group create a chart of the service project, listing what needs to be done and who is responsible. Keep the chart posted during the entire six weeks of the Lenten study.

• Worship

Before worship:

- designate one or more people to present a shell during the worship song
- ask a volunteer to read Matthew 3:17 at the appropriate time
- with the participants, begin a prayer list or a prayer chain of concerns of the group; this will be used for an opening prayer

Open the worship time with a prayer for the items on the prayer list.

Have the volunteer read Matthew 3:17.

Say: Today we have learned about Jesus, God's beloved Son. The shell is one of the symbols of baptism—Jesus' baptism and our own baptism. We present these shells as a symbol of baptism.

During the playing of an appropriate baptismal hymn or song of your choice, have the shells brought forward and laid on the worship table.

Pray: God, the source of our hope, we rededicate ourselves to our own baptisms and to the meaning of baptism. Help us to better exemplify in our lives what hope means. Amen.

Lenten Study - Week 2

Bible: Matthew 4:1-11—Jesus Is Tempted

• Arrival Activity: Temptation Test
You will need:
> large sheet of paper and marker or chalkboard and chalk
> paper
> pens or pencils

Before the session list on a large sheet of paper or chalkboard ten temptations that would be relevant to the age group(s) that are part of the study. For example: copying another person's paper for school; drinking and driving; using put-downs toward other people; not declaring cash income on your tax return; and so forth. (Number the list of temptations.)

Ask each person as he or she arrives to number a paper from 1 to 10. Then ask each person to rank the ten temptations by how much of a temptation it is for them. Have them use these rating categories: *not a chance*; *not much*; *somewhat*; *tempted*; *very tempted*.

Use these questions for discussion:
> What kinds of temptations seem more serious to you?
> Why are these temptations more serious?
> What makes it easy to avoid some temptations and difficult to avoid others?
> Is being tempted to do something wrong the same as doing it? Why or why not?

• Opening Activity: My Temptations?
Divide the participants into groups. Ask everyone to take a moment and think silently about the temptations that they face (temptations will vary from person to person). Ask each person to write or draw one of his or her temptations. Let them share within their groups, as they are willing, one or more of their own temptations.

• Bible Activity 1: Dramatize the Story
Option 1: Divide into your groups and have each group come up with a way to dramatize the Bible story, Matthew 4:1-11.

Option 2: Have one group work on preparing a dramatization of today's Bible story while other groups work on the Lenten mural (see page 85) and/or the Lenten tree (see pages 102 and 103). When everyone has finished, bring them back together and have the drama group present today's Bible story.

Explain to the participants that Jesus' temptation is not part of the Lenten story itself, but the story shows us that despite great temptation, Jesus did only the will of God. This story starts Jesus off on his ministry, which leads him down the road to his death and resurrection. It is the story of Jesus' forty days in the wilderness that are linked symbolically to the forty days of Lent—our forty days in the wilderness.

• Bible Activity 2: Lenten Cross
Add to the Lenten Cross (see page 84).

• **Craft Activity 1: Lenten Mural**
Continue working on the Lenten Mural (see page 85).

• **Craft Activity 2: Lenten Tree**
Continue working on the Lenten tree (see pages 102 and 103).

• **Game 1: Floor Game**
Continue Preparation for Floor Game (see pages 88 and 89).

• **Game 2: Making Choices Charades**
Working in their ongoing groups, have each group decide on two situations where they have to make choices (for example, to smoke or not, to cheat on a test, to blame someone else for something they have done, and so forth). Bring the groups together and let each group act out their choices in pantomime for the other groups, who are to guess what is the choice to be made.

Use the situations presented to discuss what would be a good choice, what would be a bad choice, and why.

• **Service Activity: Lenten Service Project**
Take the next step in preparation of your Lenten service project. Make sure that everyone has their assignments and that they are working on them. Be sure to contact (if necessary) whatever agency you are going to be helping so that you will help in ways that are truly needed.

• **Worship:**
Before worship:
    - designate one person to present an open Bible (the Word of God for all) during the song
    - ask a volunteer to read Matthew 4:4
    - update the prayer list or prayer chain

Open the worship time with a prayer for the items on the prayer list.

Have the volunteer read Matthew 4:4.

Say: Today we have learned how Jesus was tempted in the wilderness. Jesus was able to resist temptation because he always remained loyal to the Word of God. We too wish to keep God's Word before us.

During the playing of an appropriate hymn or song, have the Bible brought forward and laid on the worship table ("Thy Word Is a Lamp Unto My Feet" would be appropriate).

Pray: God, the source of all of our wisdom and our strength against temptation, be with us this week as we are tempted by all of the many distractions surrounding us. Help us not to forget you in the midst of all of the noise, the electronic toys, and the rich bounty around us. Help us discern your will in all we do. Amen.

Lenten Study - Week 3

- **Arrival Activity: Healing Stations**

Use the Healing Stations activity on page 87.

- **Bible Activity 1: Play Freeze!**

Use the Play Freeze! activity on pages 97 and 98.

Ask for volunteers to play each of the characters in the stories. They will need to read over their parts before you begin.

- **Bible Activity 2: Lenten Cross**

Add to the Lenten Cross (see page 84).

- **Craft Activity 1: Lenten Mural**

Continue working on the Lenten Mural (see page 85).

- **Craft Activity 2: Lenten Tree**

Continue working on the Lenten tree (see pages 102 and 103).

- **Game 1: Floor Game**

Continue Preparation for Floor Game (see pages 88 and 89).

- **Game 2: Bound and Gagged**

You will need to make photocopies of the directions on the bottom of page 86—one copy for each participating group. Be sure to cut the directions from the rest of the page. (DO NOT hand out the explanation at the top of the page.)

- **Service Activity: Continue Lenten Service Project**

Take the next step in preparation of your Lenten service project. Make sure that everyone has their own assignments and that they are working on them. Update the chart you made in Week 1 as needed.

- **Worship:**
Before worship:
- designate one person to present a roll of bandages or a box of adhesive bandages during worship
- ask a volunteer to read Matthew 8:13a
- update your prayer list or prayer chain

Open the worship time with a prayer for the items on the prayer list. This week be sure to pray specifically for those in special need of healing.

Have the volunteer read Matthew 8:13a.

Say: Today we have learned about how Jesus healed. Let us lift up our own need for healing of the body and of the spirit.

During the playing of an appropriate hymn or song, have the roll of bandages or the box of adhesive bandages brought forward and laid on the worship table.

Pray: God, the source of all healing, help us recognize our need for your healing love and care. Help strengthen our faith as we go about our daily lives. Amen.

Lenten Study - Week 4

Bible: Matthew 21:1-11—Jesus' Triumphal Entry Into Jerusalem

Note: This week's study may come before Palm Sunday, depending upon what day of the week your study is meeting and whether or not you intend to meet during Holy Week. However, Palm Sunday must be studied before the story of Holy Week itself. It's okay to study Palm Sunday now and then to celebrate it during the worship service that takes place on the actual date.

• Arrival Activity: Make Puppets on a Stick
You will need:
> construction paper
> markers or crayons
> sticks
> scissors
> glue

Give everyone a sheet of construction paper and a stick (a large craft stick will do, or you could give them sticks from small tree branches gathered from the yard). Have them draw a picture of the face of someone who might have been in the crowd to greet Jesus. Ask them to think about what the person would have been feeling. Would they be a follower? Would they have been one of the Roman authorities who thought of Jesus as a nuisance? Would they have been a religious leader there to observe and therefore fearful of what Jesus represented? Have them draw the face of their puppet to represent that feeling. They are then to cut out the face and glue it onto the stick. Use these to dramatize the story (see Bible Activity 1 below).

• Opening Activity: Who's the Leader?
Have everyone sit in a circle, and ask a volunteer to be "It." The person who is "It" leaves the room. The group then decides on a leader. The leader will lead the group in actions that the whole group will do, changing actions periodically. People are to watch the person across from them in the circle to know when to change their action, but they should try not to stare at the leader (except for the person immediately across from the leader). The leader starts one action and the volunteer "It" returns to the room. The group continues to change actions quickly and smoothly while "It" tries to discover who the leader is. When "It" guesses the leader, "It" takes the leader's seat in the circle. The leader becomes "It" and leaves the room. A new leader is chosen.

Possible actions: patting knees, snapping fingers, patting head, rubbing tummy, stomping feet.

When people seem ready to finish the game, lead a discussion of how we know a true leader. What are leadership qualities? What makes a person a good leader or a bad leader? How do we know?

• Bible Activity 1: Dramatize the Bible Story
Do a dramatic reading of Matthew 21:1-11 while everyone holds their puppets on a stick. Beginning with verse 7, at the end of each verse pause and point to two or three of the participants and have them respond with what they think their character (puppet) would say. Continue to the end of verse 11.

• **Bible Activity 2: Lenten Cross**
Have each group add to the Lenten Cross (see page 84).

• **Craft Activity 1: Lenten Mural**
Continue working on the Lenten Mural (see page 85).

• **Craft Activity 2: Lenten Tree**
Continue working on the Lenten tree (see pages 102 and 103).

• **Craft Activity 3: Make Palm Frond Crosses**
Use the instructions on page 101 to make Palm Frond Crosses. Your group may wish to make enough Palm Frond Crosses to pass out to the entire congregation.

• **Game: Floor Game**
Play the Floor Game (see pages 88 and 89).

• **Service Activity: Lenten Service Project**
Continue working on your Lenten service project.

• **Worship:**
Before worship:
- designate one person to present a palm branch (either real or one you have made from construction paper)
- ask a volunteer to read Matthew 21:9
- update your prayer list or prayer chain

Open the worship time with a prayer for the items on the prayer list.

Have the volunteer read Matthew 21:9.

Say: Today we celebrated Jesus' triumphal entry into Jerusalem. Let us remember how we glorified Jesus and keep this in our hearts and lives through the week.

During the playing of an appropriate Palm Sunday hymn or song, have the palm branch brought forward and laid on the worship table.

Pray: God, the source of our greatest joys and triumphs, be with us as we look forward to celebrating the triumph of Palm Sunday. All glory to you our Lord! Hallelujah. Amen!

Lenten Study - Week 5

Bible: Matthew 21:12–27:66—Jesus Cleansing the Temple to Jesus' Crucifixion

Note: Today's lesson covers a tremendous amount of material. You may wish to divide these learnings among the groups and then let them share what they have learned.

• Arrival Activity: Learn to Sign a Bible Verse
Before the session make photocopies of Sign a Bible Verse on page 93, or enlarge the page and post the enlarged copy where it is easily seen. As participants arrive, help them learn the signs to the Bible verse (Matthew 27:54) for use later in worship.

• Opening Activity: Make Mola Crosses
Instructions for this activity are on page 94. You will need to make photocopies of the crosses on pages 95 and 96 before the session.

• Bible Activity 1: Crucifixion Clock
Instructions for this activity are on page 104. Before the session make a photocopy of the Crucifixion Clock on page 105.

• Bible Activity 2: Lenten Cross
Add to the Lenten Cross (see page 84).

• Craft Activity 1: Lenten Mural
Continue working on the Lenten Mural (see page 85).

• Craft Activity 2: Lenten Tree
Continue working on the Lenten tree (see pages 102 and 103).

• Game: Floor Game
Play the Floor Game (see pages 88 and 89).

• Service Activity: Lenten Service Project
Continue working on your Lenten service project.

• Worship:
Before worship:
- designate one person to present a Holy Week symbol (your choice) during worship
- choose seven people and have each prepare to read one of the Scriptures listed under The Seven Last Words of Jesus (see page 79). If you have fewer than seven people, alternate readers.
- update your prayer list or prayer chain
- take a nail and hammer and tap the nail into a board, just enough for it to hold
- designate someone with a strong arm to hit the nail with the hammer during The Seven Last Words of Jesus

Open the worship time with a prayer for the items on the prayer list.

Together sign Matthew 27:54 in American Sign Language.

During the playing of an appropriate Good Friday hymn or song have a Holy Week symbol brought forward and laid on the worship table.

Darken the room slightly. Instruct the group that they are to leave in silence after the reading of the Scripture under The Seven Last Words of Jesus (see below). (They are to read John 19:26-27 in its entirety.) Have a board with a large nail and hammer. Have the nail already started in the board. Have someone with a strong arm hit the nail with the hammer once after each of the first six of The Seven Last Words of Jesus is read. After the reader says "Into your hands I commend my spirit," sit in silence for a moment.

Quietly say, "Amen."

The Seven Last Words of Jesus

• "Father, forgive them; for they do not know what they are doing." (Luke 23:34)

• "Today you will be with me in Paradise." (Luke 23:43)

• "Woman, here is your son."…"Here is your mother." (John 19:26-27)

• "My God, my God, why have you forsaken me?" (Matthew 27:46; Mark 15:34)

• "I am thirsty." (John 19:28)

• "It is finished." (John 19:30)

• "Into your hands I commend my spirit." (Luke 23:46)

Note: If you would like to have these words signed as well as read, you may find these signs on pages 41-46 of *Signs of Faith*, published by Abingdon Press.

Lenten Study - Week 6

Bible: Matthew 28; Mark 16:1-8; Luke 24:1-12; John 20:1-10—Jesus Is Raised From the Dead

• Arrival Activity 1: Take Down Lenten Symbols
As participants arrive have them strip the room of all of the symbols of Lent (including the Lenten mural). Leave only the Lenten crosses posted on the wall.

• Arrival Activity 2: Make Promise Butterflies
Have the participants use the instructions on page 113 to make butterflies as soon as they arrive in order to give the butterflies time to dry. When the butterflies are dry have participants tie them to what was the Lenten tree; it is now the Easter tree.

• Alternative or Additional Arrival Activity 1: Make Easter Flowers
You could attach colorful Easter flowers to your Easter Tree in place of (or along with) the Promise Butterflies. (The instructions are on page 116.)

• Alternative or Additional Arrival Activity 2: Live Easter Flowers
Attach live flowers to your Easter Tree or to an empty cross.

• Bible Activity: Scrambled Eggs

This activity is described on pages 114 and 115. It requires advanced preparation. You will need to gather the plastic eggs, make photocopies of the Bible verses, cut them apart, put them in the eggs, and hide the eggs—all before the session.

• Game: Floor Game
Play the Floor Game (see pages 88 and 89).

• Service Activity: Complete Lenten Service Project
If you have not already done so, complete your Lenten service project.

• Party
Have a party—serve refreshments, play games, and generally have a good time.

• Worship:
Bring the group together for worship by playing the liveliest Easter music available to you. If you have someone to play and lead music let people choose their favorite Easter hymns and sing them together. They only get to sing them once each year.

Say a prayer for all the subjects on your ongoing prayer list or prayer chain.

Close with everyone saying the Lord's Prayer together.

Activity: Water Stations

Water is the main symbol of baptism. To set the tone for a session on baptism, have a learning center with stations set up where people can experience and think about water and its importance.

You will need:
 tub of water   towels
 cassette of recorded water sounds tub or bucket of sand
 cassette player   old newspaper or plastic
 real shells or shell molds   water toys (optional)
 directions and supplies for making a drinking fountain

Play in Water
Have a tub of water and some towels available. Include instructions at this station for participants to play in the water and to describe to one other person his or her own baptism. You may wish to have water toys available at this station.

Listen and Draw
Before the session record sounds of water such as a fountain, water running from a tap, someone splashing in water, and a dishwasher or washing machine running. Place a sign in this station asking participants to listen to the sounds of water and then draw a picture depicting what water "sounds" like to them.

Symbols of Baptism

Spread out old newspaper or sheets of plastic. Have a tub or buckets of sand and some water. Ask participants to make sand shells by mixing sand and water and molding it using shells or shell molds. They will need to get the sand the right consistency to hold a shape—just like making a sand castle. Have a large sheet of paper or plastic where the molds can be turned over and the sand shells can be displayed. (Remember these symbols are temporary—just like any sand sculpture you make at the seashore.)

Church Water Fountain
Find instructions and parts at a local hardware store and have participants work together to make a small, working water fountain for the church.

Water Experiment
Set up the water experiment Long Distance Pouring (see page 82) or substitute a water experiment of your choice.

Activity: Long Distance Pouring

You will need:

> pitcher
> drinking glass

> string
> food coloring (optional)

Have available an empty glass, a pitcher half-filled with water, and a piece of string about 18 inches long. (To make this easier to see as well as more dramatic, add a few drops of food coloring to the water.)

You may demonstrate this activity yourself or write out the following directions for those working in learning stations without a leader:

1. ***Wet the piece of string thoroughly.*** Then tie one end of the string to the handle of the pitcher and stretch it very tightly across the top of the spout. Let the other end of the string fall into the glass.

2. With one hand, hold the pitcher by the handle approximately 1 foot above and 2 feet away from the glass. At the same time, with your other hand, hold the end of the string firmly against the inside of the glass.

3. SLOWLY pour the water down the string. The water should cling to the already-wet string and slowly start to fill the glass.

    This may take a couple of tries to get the angle right.

Activity: Group-Building Game

You will need:

    cup
    shell
    other objects as desired (optional)

Have participants sit in a circle. Have two or more objects that you can pass (depending upon size of group and time). For a baptism theme you might use a paper cup (representing water) and a shell.

Sit in the chair with the participants. You will be person 1. You will pass the shell to the person on your left (person 2), saying, "This is a shell." The shell should be passed as quickly (and as rhythmically) as possible, moving from person to person around the circle as follows:

    Person 1:   This is a shell.
    Person 2:   A what?
    Person 1.   A shell.
    Person 2:   A what?
    Person 1:   A shell.
    Person 2:   A what?
    Person 1:   A shell.
    Person 2:   Oh! A shell!

Person 2 then takes the shell and passes it to person 3 saying, "This is a shell," and persons 2 and 3 repeat the formula. (Notice that each person asks "a what" three times.) Continue all the way around the circle. Start the game again with the shell moving to the left. Then immediately begin the same process with the cup going to the right. There will be a lot of fun and confusion when the two items meet.

Note: If you want to create more confusion and laughter start a third and/or fourth object around the circle.

Activity: Lenten Cross

You will need:
    construction paper   markers
    masking tape or pushpins

Session 1—Divide participants into groups. Each group will use seven sheets of 8½- by 11-inch construction paper to construct a cross to hang on the wall or bulletin board. The group will add one piece of paper to their cross each week.

Have each group decide on a Communion symbol to draw on a sheet of construction paper. Then have them post that sheet on the wall or bulletin board. Ask each group to decide on a name for their group and then write that name on another piece of construction paper. Have them post their name close to the paper they have already posted. This designates their area for their cross.

At the end of the study the crosses will be laid out like this:

	Week 6			Group Name
Week 5	Week 3	Week 4		
	Week 2			
	Week 1			

Session 2—Have participants work in their ongoing groups. Ask each group to draw on one of their sheets of construction paper a scroll, a Bible, or another symbol that they think represents the Word of God. (Remember that Jesus bases his resistance to temptation on the Word of God.) Then have them post that sheet on the wall to make part 2 of their cross.

Session 3—For session 3 have the groups draw a bandage (or something representing healing) on their sheet of construction paper and add that sheet to their cross on the wall.

Session 4—For session 4 have the groups draw palm leaves (or something else representing Palm Sunday) on their sheet of construction paper and add that sheet to their cross on the wall.

Session 5—For session 5 have the groups choose one of the many symbols of Holy Week to draw on their sheet of construction paper—a crown of thorns; three crosses (for Jesus and the two thieves); a whip; a sign saying, "King of the Jews"; and so forth. Then have them add their sheet to the cross.

Session 6—This section of the construction paper cross should be the top section of the cross. Have each group decide on a Resurrection symbol with which they wish to finish their cross—a butterfly, a phoenix rising from the ashes, a lily, flowers of all kinds, an egg cracked open, a peacock, or a pomegranate.

Activity: Lenten Mural

You will need:
   Bibles
   large sheets of posterboard or large roll of paper
   crayons or markers
   masking tape or pushpins

This will be a five-part mural for the wall or bulletin board of your room (or a wall in a prominent hallway where others can see it). Each session you will depict the story that you are studying.

The mural can be an actual depiction of events or it can be a symbolic mural.

Session 1—Let the class decide what they want to appear on the first section of the mural; let them look at today's story of Jesus' baptism (Matthew 3:13-17). Using large sheets of posterboard or a large roll of paper, let them design and color in the first section of the mural. If they desire to use symbols, the symbols for baptism are water, the shell with three drops of water, and the descending dove. It would also be appropriate to use symbols for Jesus.

Note: If you wish to know more about symbols for Jesus, refer to *Symbols of Faith*, published by Abingdon Press.

Session 2—Continuing on the large roll of paper started last week or adding a second sheet of posterboard, have the participants create a picture (or symbols) for the temptation of Jesus (Matthew 4:1-11).

Session 3—Continuing on the large roll of paper or adding a third sheet of posterboard, have the participants create a picture (or symbols) for Jesus healing a leper, Jesus healing the Centurion's servant, or Jesus healing many people at Peter's house (Matthew 8:1-17).

Note: You might assign the three different healing stories to three separate groups and assign each group one section of the posterboard or paper to decorate.

Session 4—Continuing on the large roll of paper or adding a fourth sheet of posterboard, have the participants create a picture (or symbols) of Jesus' triumphal entry into Jerusalem (Matthew 21:1-11).

Session 5—Continuing on the large roll of paper or adding a fifth sheet of posterboard, have the participants create a picture (or symbols) for the arrest, trial, and crucifixion of Jesus (Matthew 21:11–27:66). Divide the different parts of the story among different groups for illustration.

Activity: Bound and Gagged

You will need:

two or more large sheets of paper
pieces of cloth

masking tape or pushpins
markers

Before the session post two or more large sheets of paper at one end of the room. Do not tell the participants what you are going to do with the paper. Divide the participants into two or more teams (one for each sheet of paper).

Say: We're going to play a game in which you will all be bound in some way. I will give each team written instructions as to what you are to do.

Very gently bind participants with large pieces of cloth in the following ways: blindfold one (this person cannot see); put a gag on one (this person is not allowed to talk); bind another's arms to his or her sides (this person is not allowed to use his or her hands); bind one's feet together (this person cannot walk); and wrap a cloth around one person's ears (this person cannot be spoken to; communication must be done in another form).

Note: Five is the perfect number for a team. But if you have fewer than that number per team, you can bind participants in more than one way. For example, the person who is gagged could also have his or her ears bound. If you have more than five per group, either subdivide the groups or bind two people in a group in the same way.

Say: Each of you is bound in a different way. This binding limits one of the tasks that you can do. Together you must accomplish the task I will give your team. The only way to complete the task is to work together.

Place the teams at the end of the room opposite the large sheets of paper you posted. Put felt-tip markers close to the paper. Ask the person in each group who is gagged and not allowed to speak to come and get the directions from you. Give each team a photocopy of the directions below. Stand back and see how each group decides to accomplish their task. (The person who is gagged is allowed to show the directions to other team members.) When all groups have completed the task, bring them back together to discuss their experience.

Directions:

Together everybody in your group needs to get to the other end of the room. There you will find a large sheet of paper. On that paper draw a large triangle. Inside the triangle draw a circle. On one side of the triangle write the word "God." On the second side of the triangle write "Jesus," and on the third side of the triangle write "Holy Spirit."

Each member of your group must sign his or her own name to the paper.

Remember, you are NOT allowed to use the part of your body that is tied.

Seasons of Faith

Activity: Healing Stations

Set up a learning center and have participants choose from among these healing stations that will help them think about healing in many different ways.

You will need:

CD and CD player	objects related to healing
tray	towel
plastic foam cups	glue
old newspapers and magazines	posterboard
paper	pens or pencils
markers	terra cotta pots (optional)

Soothing Sounds

Have a CD player available and play a CD of soft, soothing music. Or before the session record soothing sounds such as a wind chime blowing in the breeze, flowing water, a rainstick, and muted chiming of a church bell. Have participants close their eyes, listen to the sounds, and think about what is good in their lives.

Identify Objects

Gather objects related to healing, place them on a tray, and cover them with a towel so that they can be felt but not seen. Ask people to feel the objects and list on a sheet of paper what they think is under the towel. (No hints please. Do NOT tell them that they are healing objects.) Ask them to sign their paper, fold it, and place it in the station. After everyone has had a chance to go through the station, reveal what the objects are. Have everyone check their papers to see who came closest.

Possible healing objects: box of bandage strips; roll of bandages; thermometer; bottle of pills; Bible (representing faith); bottle of cough syrup and spoon; and if you know a doctor or nurse, he or she might lend you a stethoscope.

Mend Me

Place plastic foam cups and a bottle of glue on a table. Have directions available stating to take one cup and tear it into pieces. Then direct them to use the glue to put the pieces back together. On a piece of posterboard labeled "New Uses," have them write one thing for which the new cup could be used (for example, it could be used for potting a small plant if put inside another container—it would drain well when watered, or it could be painted and used as a decoration, or it could be used as a mold for a sand sculpture).

Note: You could do this with terra cotta pots and a stronger glue. You could also give them the option of making "mosaics" instead of putting the cup or pot back together.

Make a Healing Collage

Have old newspapers and magazines available. Have people search for pictures and/or stories that show healing (of the body, mind, or spirit), and glue them to a large posterboard.

Activity: Holy Week and Easter floor Game

You will need:

Bibles
index cards
photocopy of pages 90-92
masking tape
boxes (optional)
chairs (optional)

several colors of construction paper
markers
scissors
tables and/or blocks (optional)
posterboard (optional)
plant or tree for the Mount of Olives (optional)

Have everyone work together to start creating one giant board game that is played using the entire room as the "board" for the game. The game will actually be played in the last two sessions of the Lenten study.

Session 1—Use the sample on page 89 for an idea of a layout for your floor game. Establish what the general "route" of the gameboard will be. How many sheets of construction paper will you need? Exactly where will you put Bethany, the Mount of Olives, the two city gates, the Temple, Pontius Pilate's place, the Upper Room, Golgotha, and the tomb? Have someone sketch this plan so it will be remembered when it is time for the final set up for play.

Session 2—Together decide which squares you will designate as question squares (every fourth, every fifth, random squares?). When a player lands on a question square, they are asked a question (see pages 90-92). Decide which if any squares will hold "dangers" (for example, running into thieves or getting lost). What will happen when a player lands on a danger square? Will the player lose a turn, go back two spaces, or another option? Count out the number of pieces of paper to be labeled and assign individuals to label them. (They may wish to designate them by drawing Holy Week symbols on the designated question squares.) Have them list the rules on a large sheet of posterboard.

Session 3—Decide on the rules of the game. How will you decide how many spaces to move? Will you play as individuals or groups? Will one person be the designated "moving piece" for his or her group? Will they rotate which group member answers a question or will the entire group have to agree on the answer? Will there be time limits to answering?

Session 4—Using the game cards and Bible quickly go over the events of Holy Week with the participants. (This prepares them to play in the next session.)

Session 5—Before the session make a photocopy of the question cards on pages 90-92 and cut them apart. Pull out those cards having to do with everything from Palm Sunday through the Crucifixion. (You will add the question cards about the Resurrection at the next session.) Mix the cards up. Have the person who made the sketch of your floor gameboard direct everyone in setting up the game—placing the objects you have chosen for city gates, and so forth, where they belong. You will want to tape the construction paper pieces to the floor. Post the rules of the game and play.

Session 6—Again lay out your game. Make sure rules are posted. Add the Resurrection cards and play.

Variation—Have participants make question cards from the Lenten study.

What was one kind of teaching Jesus did while in Jerusalem?

He taught many parables.
(Matthew 21:33–22:14; Matthew 24:45–25:46)

What is the name of the Jewish festival that Jesus and the disciples were celebrating in the Upper Room?

Passover. (Matthew 26:19)

Who does Jesus predict will betray him?

Judas. (Matthew 26:24-25)

Where did Jesus go to pray after the Passover meal?

Gethsemane. (Matthew 26:36)

What animal did Jesus ride into Jerusalem?

A donkey. (Matthew 21:2)

What did the crowds say when Jesus entered Jerusalem?

"Hosanna to the Son of David! Blessed is the one who comes in the name of the Lord! Hosanna in the highest heaven!" (Matthew 21:9)

Who did Jesus drive away from the Temple?

Those who were selling and buying in the Temple.
(Matthew 21:12)

After throwing the merchants out of the Temple, what did Jesus say the Temple should be called?

A house of prayer. (Matthew 21:13)

What choice did Pilate offer to the crowd?

"Whom do you want me to release for you, Jesus Barabbas or Jesus who is called the Messiah?" (Matthew 27:17)

Who mocked Jesus?

The Roman soldiers. (Matthew 27:27-31)

Who was compelled to carry Jesus' cross?

Simon the Cyrene. (Matthew 27:32)

What happened at the moment Jesus died?

The curtain of the Temple was torn in two, the earth shook, the rocks split, and the tombs were opened. (Matthew 27:51-52)

What did the disciples do while Jesus prayed in Gethsemane?

Slept. (Matthew 26:40)

Where was Jesus taken after he was arrested?

To Caiaphas, the High Priest. (Matthew 26:57)

Who denied knowing Jesus after his arrest?

Peter. (Matthew 26:69-75)

What did Pilate ask Jesus?

"Are you the King of the Jews?" (Matthew 27:11)

Who first announced that Jesus had risen?

An angel. (Matthew 28:2-6)

As the women ran to tell the disciples of the Resurrection, who met them?

Jesus. (Matthew 28:9)

What did the chief priests tell those who guarded the tomb to report to the governor?

"His disciples came by night and stole him away while we were asleep." (Matthew 28:13)

After the Resurrection what did Jesus tell the disciples?

"Go therefore and make disciples of all nations, baptizing them in the name of the Father and of the Son and of the Holy Spirit." (Matthew 28:19)

Who said, "Truly this man was God's Son"?

A Roman centurion. (Matthew 27:54)

Who watched the crucifixion from a distance?

Mary Magdalene, Mary the mother of James and Joseph, and the mother of the sons of Zebedee. (Matthew 27:56)

Who asked for the body of Jesus and gave it a proper burial?

Joseph of Arimathea. (Matthew 27:57)

After the sabbath, as the first day of the week was dawning, who went to the tomb?

Mary Magdalene and the other Mary. (Matthew 28:1)

Activity: Sign a Bible Verse

Below is an illustration of how to sign Matthew 27:54 using American Sign Language.

TRULY: Hold the side of your right index finger against your lips and move it forward in an arc.

THIS: Place the tip of your right index finger into the open palm of your left hand.

MAN: With your right hand, grasp the brim of an imaginary hat as shown; then bring the flat hand, palm down, away from your head at forehead level.

WAS: Raise the right hand to the right side of the face, palm facing the body. Curve the right hand back and over the right shoulder.

GOD'S: Sign the letter "G" with the right hand with palm facing left and point forward and up at head level. Then move the right hand down and back toward the body ending with an open palm facing left at chest level.

SON: Salute with your right hand as shown; then bring the same hand down until it rests in the crook of your bent left arm with both palms facing up.

Activity: Mola Crosses

On the San Blas Islands, near the eastern coast of the country of Panama in Central America, live the Cuna people. The Cuna are known for creating beautiful designs. They embroider overlays of bright cloth on their clothing. These are called mola designs.

You may use one of three options for making mola crosses.
You will need:

pencils	photocopy of the cross designs on pages 95-96
scissors	glue
(option one) three different colors of construction paper	
(option two) three different colors of felt	
(option three) scrap pieces of cloth and needle and thread	

Option One (for younger children or for a quick activity)
Have participants select one of the cross patterns and use it to trace the cross on three different colors of construction paper. They are to make the cross slightly larger each time they trace the cross.

Cut out the crosses. Glue them on top of one another, with the largest one on the bottom and the smallest one on the top. Only the outside edges of the bottom two crosses will show, but you will be able to see all of the smallest cross.

Option Two
Instead of using construction paper and glue, use felt and glue. Proceed as above.

Option Three
Instead of construction paper or felt, use scrap pieces of cloth and needle and thread. Proceed as above only hand sew the crosses together to make true mola crosses.

Seasons of Faith

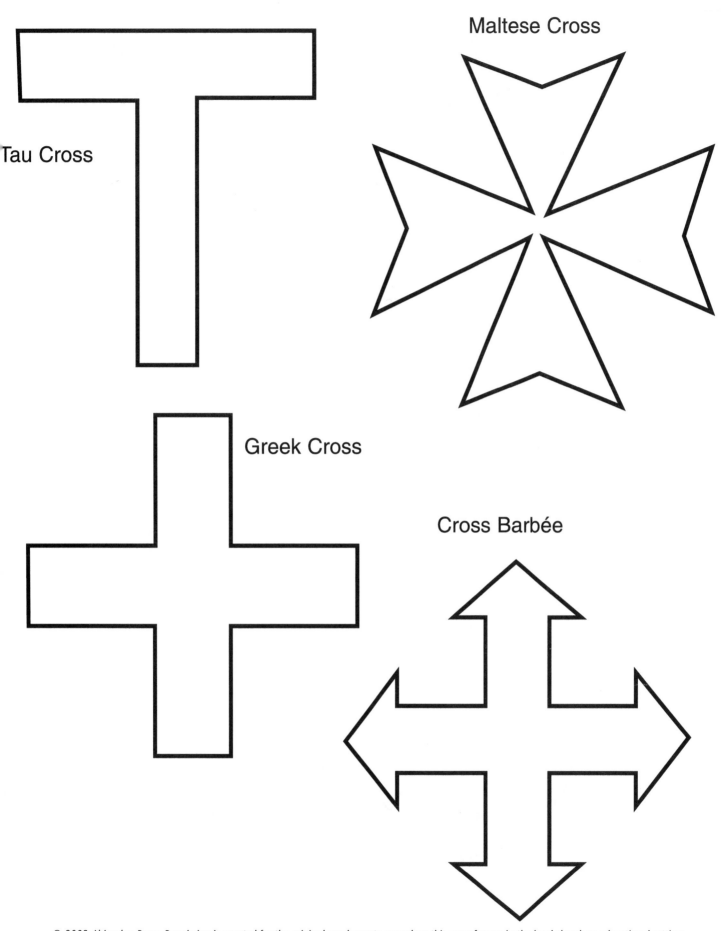

Tau Cross

Maltese Cross

Greek Cross

Cross Barbée

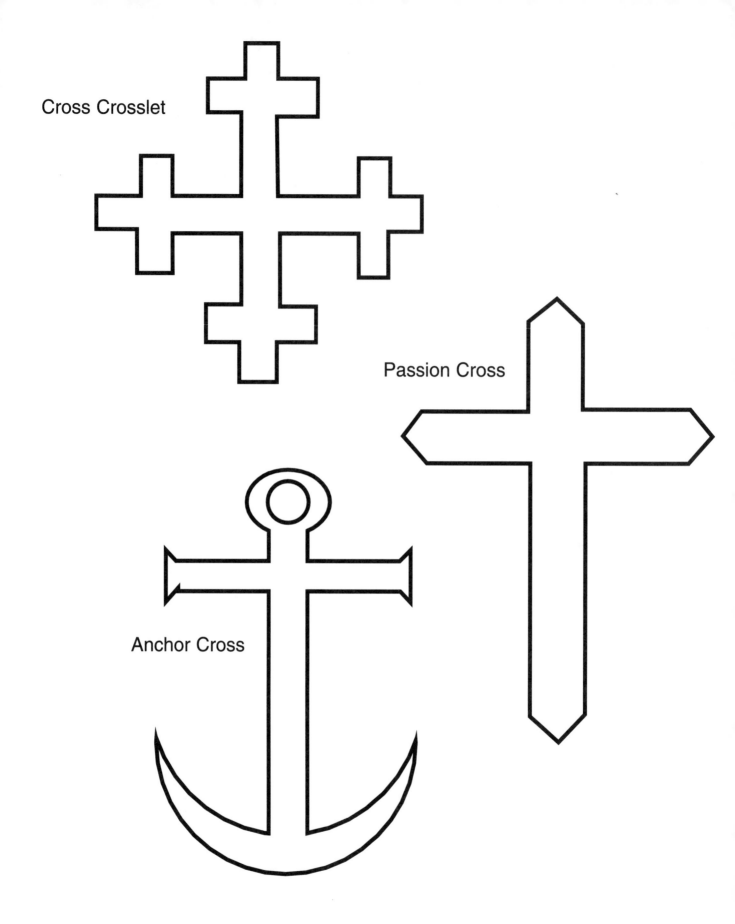

Cross Crosslet

Passion Cross

Anchor Cross

Seasons of Faith

Activity: Play Freeze!

You will need:

Bibles
bell
video camera (optional)
television and VCR (optional)

photocopies of the three Bible stories (pages 97-98)
simple costumes (optional)
blank videocassette tape (optional)

Ask for volunteers to play each of the characters in the three Bible stories. They will need to read over their parts before beginning. When you come to the word *Freeze!* in the script, ring the bell and have the actors freeze in words and actions—even if it's in the middle of a sentence. While the actors are "frozen," discuss with the rest of the class what has just happened, what the words or actions mean, and so forth. After the discussion, say *"Unfreeze!"* and continue.

Note: An option would be to make a video recording of the three plays, then play the tape back and *"Freeze"* the tape for your discussion.

Freeze Story One—Jesus Cleanses a Leper (Matthew 8:1-4)

Narrator: Jesus has come down from the mountain. Great crowds are following him, and the leper is among them.

Leper: *(kneeling before Jesus)* Lord, if you choose, you can make me clean.
Freeze! Wait a minute. What is this leper doing in town? This person is not clean. He should be outside the town limits, removed from the community. The leper took the initiative to get Jesus to help him. His faith was strong. He knew that Jesus could heal him; the question was, would Jesus choose to heal him? *Unfreeze!*

Jesus: *(Stretches out hand and touches leper)*
Freeze! Jesus touched an unclean person. This action broke the Jewish law about coming in direct contact with unclean people. By touching this unclean person, Jesus, by Jewish law, was now unclean himself. *Unfreeze!*

Jesus: I do choose. Be made clean!
(The leprosy was healed. Former leper jumps up filled with joy.)
Freeze! The touch that made Jesus ritually unclean was the condition for the cleansing. *Unfreeze!*

Jesus: See that you say nothing to anyone; but go, show yourself to the priest, and offer the gift that Moses commanded, as a testimony to them.
Freeze! A person cured of leprosy had to undergo purification rituals at the Temple before he or she would be allowed to enter back into the community. Jesus told the leper to go through the ritual process that would make it possible for the former leper to return to his community. *Unfreeze!*

Activity: Play Freeze! (Continued)

Narrator: Jesus enters Capernaum; a centurion comes to him appealing for his servant to be healed.
Freeze! Gentiles lived in Capernaum; this was not a Jewish community. *Unfreeze!*

Centurion: Lord,
Freeze! By saying "Lord" the centurion was humbling himself before Jesus. The soldier was the advocate for someone who had no power—his servant. *Unfreeze!*

Centurion: my servant is lying at home paralyzed, in terrible distress.

Jesus: I will come and cure him.

Centurion: Lord, I am not worthy to have you come under my roof; but only speak the word, and my servant will be healed.
Freeze! The centurion's faith was strong. The centurion embodied the faith that Jesus wanted his followers to have. *Unfreeze!*

Centurion: For I also am a man under authority, with soldiers under me; and I say to one, "Go," and he goes, and to another, "Come," and he comes, and to my slave, "Do this," and the slave does it.

Jesus: *(turning to his followers, a look of amazement on his face)* Truly I tell you, in no one in Israel have I found such faith. I tell you, many will come from east and west and will eat with Abraham and Isaac and Jacob in the kingdom of heaven, while the heirs of the kingdom will be thrown into the outer darkness, where there will be weeping and gnashing of teeth. *(facing the Centurion)* Go; let it be done for you according to your faith.

Narrator: The servant was healed in that hour.

Freeze Story Three—Jesus Heals Peter's Mother-in-law (Matthew 8:14-17)

Narrator 1: Jesus enters Peter's house and sees Peter's mother-in-law lying in bed with a fever.

Jesus: *(touches Peter's mother in-law)*
Freeze! There goes Jesus touching the unclean again. The Jewish religious leaders were not pleased with his healing technique. *Unfreeze!*

Narrator 1: The fever left her.

Mother-in-law: *(Rise. Kneel before Jesus, then go attend other sick people.)*

Narrator 1: She got up and began to serve Jesus.
Freeze! The healing of Peter's mother-in-law became her call to ministry. Jesus healed her. In that healing she was restored to the community. As a response she began to serve Jesus. *Unfreeze!*

Narrator 2: That evening they brought to [Jesus] many who were possessed with demons; and he cast out the spirits with a word, and cured all who were sick. This was to fulfill what had been spoken through the prophet Isaiah, "He took our infirmities and bore our diseases."

Activity: Lenten Calendar

You will need:

pencils or markers   up-to-date calendar
photocopies of blank monthly Lenten calendar form (see page 100)

For each participant make two or three copies of the blank monthly Lenten calendar form on page 100. (The number of copies will depend on in what month Ash Wednesday occurs and in what month Easter occurs. For example, in 2004 Ash Wednesday is on February 25 and Easter is on April 11; the participants will need three months for their 2004 Lenten calendar.)

Give the participants the following instructions.

1. Date your calendar forms with the correct dates for each day in the Lenten season.

2. Find the date of Ash Wednesday. (Unsure of dates? Use the chart on page 10.) Mark that date on the calendar.

3. Find the dates of Holy Thursday (also known as Maundy Thursday), Good Friday, and Easter Sunday. Mark these dates on your calendar.

4. Mark each of the Sundays "Worship." Explain that Sundays are not counted as part of the forty days of Lent because each Sunday is a small celebration of the resurrection of Christ.

5. Ask them to work in their groups to decide what each member of the group is going to do each day of Lent (it is okay for the groups to do different things). Have them either choose from the following list or suggest ideas of their own. Then have them record one of the activities on each square of their Lenten calendars (excluding Sundays).

   • Bible reading—use the Holy Week stories, Psalms, Proverbs, and other favorite Bible passages.
   • Ideas for serving God—helping a neighbor, cleaning up someone's yard, saving money to give to a charity, and so forth.
   • Prayer—set aside times for prayer during each week.
   • Journaling—write something each day about what is happening in their spiritual lives.
   • Calling others in their study group to see how they are doing.

The groups will be responsible for holding each other accountable for completing what is on their Lenten calendars.

Sunday	Monday	Tuesday	Wednesday	Thursday	Friday	Saturday

Seasons of Faith

Activity: Palm Frond Cross

You will need:

> one short palm frond (approximately 11 inches long)
> one long palm frond (approximately 14 inches long)

1. Select two palm fronds from a palm branch.

2. Fold the shorter length as shown. Flatten the small section in the middle to create a loop.

3. Cut one end of the longer palm frond into a point.

4. Put the pointed end of the longer palm frond into the loop on the shorter palm frond. (Do not pull it through the loop.)

5. Take the other end of the long palm frond (the end without a point) and push it through the loop. Pull it tight.

6. Bring the long palm frond back through the loop again. Pull it through, leaving about 2 to 2½ inches at the top.

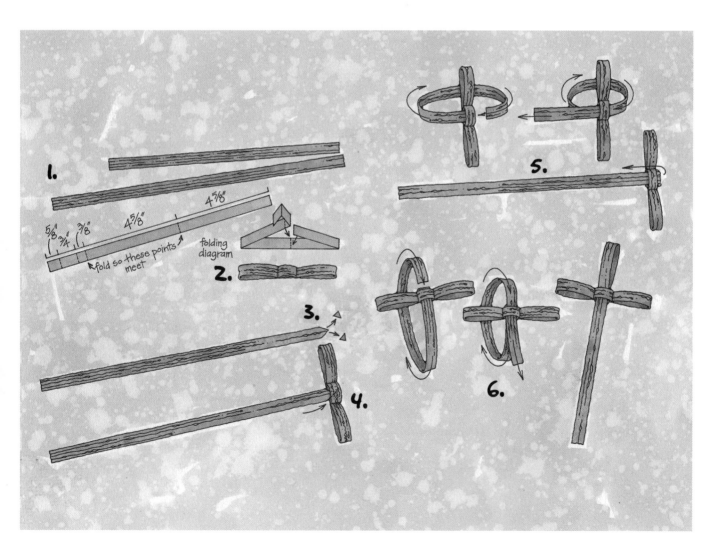

Activity: Lenten Tree

At Christmas we use an evergreen tree to depict new life. The same thing can be done during the Lenten season. The difference is that the Lenten season uses the symbols of the events of Holy Week.

Week 1: The color for Lent is purple.
You will need:

artificial or real evergreen tree	purple cloth
purple ribbon	floral wire or twist ties

Have on hand a purple cloth to be placed around the base of the tree and purple ribbon. Have participants drape the cloth around the tree base and make purple bows. Once the bows are made have them use floral wire or twist ties to attach the bows to the tree.

Week 2: The Money Bag
You will need:

nylon netting	pennies
scissors	ribbon and yarn

The money bag and coins symbolize the thirty pieces of silver Judas received for betraying Jesus (Matthew 26:14-16; Mark 14:10-11; Luke 22:3-6). To make money bags to place on the tree this week, have nylon netting available. Have the participants cut the netting into small squares and place several pennies in each square. Tie the money bags onto the Lenten tree using yarn.

Week 3: The Chalice
You will need:

small paper cups	ribbon or yarn
aluminum foil	small plastic cups used in Communion trays (optional)
tape	

During the meal in the Upper Room Jesus instituted the Lord's Supper by the sharing of bread and wine (Matthew 26:17-29; Mark 14:22-25; Luke 22:15-20). The bread represents Christ's body, and the wine, the blood of the new covenant. The chalice will be this week's symbol for the Lenten tree. Make the chalices by taping together the bottoms of two small paper cups. Cover the cups with aluminum foil, molding the foil to the contours. Punch a hole in the top of the chalice and hang it on the tree with yarn.

Option: If you have a lot of the small plastic cups used often in Communion trays, punch a hole near the top of the cups, string purple yarn or ribbon through the hole, and hang them from the tree.

Week 4: The Pretzel
You will need:
    pretzels   purple ribbon or yarn

The pretzel was created as a symbol of praying hands. In the Garden of Gethsemane Christ prayed (Matthew 26:36-46; Mark 14:32-42; Luke 22:39-46).

Have participants tie purple yarn or ribbon through the pretzels and hang them on the tree in remembrance.

Week 5: The Nail
You will need:
    nails   purple ribbon or yarn

The nail reminds us of the suffering Jesus experienced on the cross.

Have participants tie purple yarn or ribbon around the head of a nail in representation of the suffering and death of Jesus. Hang the nails on the tree.

Week 6 (or whichever week you study Palm Sunday): Palm Branches
You will need:
    live palm branches
    or
    construction paper and scissors

In celebration of Jesus' triumphal entry into Jerusalem, place live palm branches on the purple cloth at the base of the cross. (If no live palm branches are available, construct some from paper or some other material.)

Easter: Resurrection symbols
You will need:
    craft items to make Resurrection symbols
    white cloth

Make your favorite Resurrection symbols for the tree—flowers, butterflies, decorated eggs, and so forth.

Remove ALL of the Lenten symbols from the tree. Remove the purple cloth and replace it with a white cloth. White symbolizes purity and joy and is why Easter lilies are always white. Fill your Easter tree with the symbols of Resurrection that you have made.

Activity: Crucifixion clock

You will need:
- Bibles
- photocopy of Crucifixion clock (see page 105)
- glue
- paper or posterboard

Use this activity to help participants visualize the time frame of the crucifixion (all times are approximate).

Note: On the Crucifixion Clock, 3:00-5:00 P.M. is an approximation referring to the time of the slaying of the Passover lamb. Actual death of Jesus, "It is finished," is thought to be 3:00 P.M.

Make a photocopy of the Crucifixion Clock on page 105. Glue this page to another sheet of paper or a posterboard to give it strength. Very carefully cut out the inside portion of the clock leaving the circle of times intact. Tape the circle of times together where you cut it to get to the inside circle. Cut apart the pie shapes of the inner circle and mix them up.

Pass the pie pieces of the clock out to to the participants and ask them to see if they can put the clock together matching their piece of the pie to the time on the outer circle. Spend as much time as necessary putting the puzzle-clock together. Discuss the events. The related Scriptures are listed below:

6:00 A.M.—Mark 15:1-5; Luke 23:6-10

7:00 A.M.—Luke 23:11, 23-24

8:00 A.M.—Luke 23:26

9:00 A.M.—Luke 23:33

10:00 A.M.—Mark 15:24; Luke 23:34

11:00 A.M.—Luke 23:39, 43

12:00 P.M.—John 19:26-27; Mark 15:33

1:00 P.M.—Matthew 27:46

2:00 P.M.—John 19:28

3:00 P.M.—John 19:30; Luke 23:46

4:00 P.M.—Matthew 27:51

5:00 P.M.—Matthew 27:52; John 19:34

After the clock has been put together, you might have volunteers read the relevant Scriptures.

Crucifixion Clock

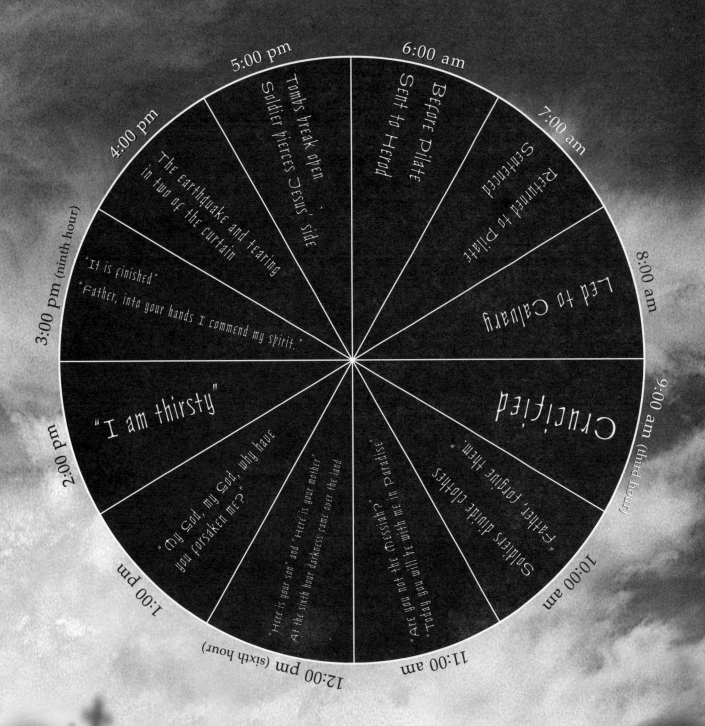

Holy Week— The Three Great Days

Most Christians are familiar with the season and services of Holy Week—a time of remembrance of the last days of Jesus. Over time services came to commemorate the events of the last week of Jesus' life, and each of the services is meant to lead us through the real and painful events leading up to the death and resurrection of Jesus the Christ.

Holy (Maundy) Thursday—Maundy probably comes from the Latin word meaning "mandate" (commandment). It refers to the story in John 13:1-20 where Jesus washes the feet of the disciples and tells them they ought to follow his example.

Some churches hold foot-washing services on Holy Thursday. Communion is also a large part of a Holy Thursday service. Sometimes worship will be a Communion service; sometimes the worship will also emphasize service to others.

Good Friday - Originally Good Friday was known as Paschal Day. Paschal is a term derived from the word "Pesakh," which is the Hebrew word for Passover. This is the day that the death and resurrection of Jesus are commemorated by the church. The term Good Friday comes from the English church. In Old English, "Good" meant "Holy," so the title Good Friday means "Holy Friday."

Traditionally Good Friday services have been held in churches from 1:00 to 3:00 in the afternoon, although in recent years more and more of these services are being held on Friday evening. Good Friday services are very often ecumenical with churches joining together to offer the Good Friday service.

In all Christian churches the Good Friday service stresses the Passion of Christ. In Protestant churches the stripping of the church of all adornment other than the cross often occurs before, during, or after this service. Often the cross is draped with a black cloth symbolizing the death of Jesus.

Holy Saturday—Holy Saturday is often viewed as the last sabbath for the disciples as Jews. It is with the resurrection of Jesus that the disciples became Christians celebrating the Resurrection on Sunday.

Some churches provide Stations of the Cross (a walk through the arrest and crucifixion of Jesus) on Holy Saturday. Other churches do nothing on this day.

"The Great Three Days from sunset Holy Thursday to sunset Easter Day are a unity—the climax of the Christian year." (The United Methodist Book of Worship)

Seasons of Faith

Easter

Easter

Many people today are under the mistaken impression that Easter Sunday is an adaptation of an ancient pagan holiday. It is true that many people feel it was named after the Anglo-Saxon spring goddess, Eastre. Some scholars now believe that the word "easter" may actually come from the German word "eostarun," which means "dawn." These scholars feel that the word is actually a mistranslation of the word "albae," which means both "dawn" and "white." The early church called Easter week hebdomada alba (white week) because of the white clothes worn by those who were baptized at Easter. If this is true then the word "easter" really means "white" (which is the liturgical color for Easter). Except for the name and some spring rites such as decorating with flowers, Easter is a scriptural and specifically Christian holiday.

By the end of the first century an annual commemoration of Jesus' resurrection had been established. It was called Pascha.

Most European languages such as Spanish, Italian, and French use words that were derived from the Greek word "Pasha," their term for the Hebrew Passover. It is looked upon as the Christian Passover—the time of deliverance of believers from the death that sin brings upon us. We are saved for eternal life.

With the exception of Sunday, always a small celebration of the Resurrection, Easter is the oldest Christian holiday.

Easter is observed on the first Sunday following the full moon that occurs on or next after March 21.

Originally there was a lot of controversy as to exactly when Easter should be celebrated. There were a lot of complicated arguments about whether it should be held on the day of the sacrifice of the lamb of the Passover (that could happen any day of the week), or whether it should be celebrated only on a Sunday because the Resurrection took place on a Sunday. The Council of Nicaea (325 A.D.) decided that Easter should always be held on Sunday. But the Eastern and the Roman churches calculated the date in different ways. By a complicated process it was decided that churches throughout the world would celebrate after March 21, the vernal equinox. The controversy went on and on for centuries until finally the day of Easter has come to be celebrated as we now know it.

Part of the controversy was over whether it was Jesus' sacrifice for us or Jesus' resurrection which needed to be celebrated. However if Christians observe the services of the days from Maundy Thursday through Easter morning worship, they will have celebrated both the sacrifice and the Resurrection.

Activity: Pysanka Eggs

Pysanka eggs were first made in the Ukraine. They were made at Easter as a way to recognize the new life that God has given us through Jesus Christ. Pysanka eggs are beautifully decorated with wax and different colors of dye.

You will need:

eggs that have not been boiled
spoon
cotton swabs
needle or pin (optional)
powdered dyes in several colors (you can use Easter-egg dyes)
kistka—to make a kistka, push a small nail into the eraser end of a pencil

short candle
bowls
ribbon (optional)
straw (optional)

Prepare the powdered dyes in jars. Light the candle and hold the nail of the kistka over the flame to heat the nail. Dip the nail end into the melted wax of the candle and draw on the egg with the wax. Do this again several times. Everywhere you put wax will remain white on the egg.

Then use a spoon to dip the egg into the lightest color of dye you have. Hold the egg in the dye for five minutes. Then remove the egg and let it dry for a few minutes. Use the nail of the kistka to apply wax to all of the areas that you want to remain the color of the dye you just used.

Dip the egg in the dye that is the second lightest color you have. Hold the egg there for five minutes, then remove it and let it dry for five minutes. Use the nail end of the kistka to apply wax to all the areas of the egg that you want to remain the second color.

Repeat the process, each time using the color that is next in order from light to dark. Let your egg dry.

You can keep your egg for a long time if you "blow out" your egg. Use a needle or a pin to make a small hole in one end. Make a larger hole in the other end. Cut a straw to about three inches in length. Put the straw over the small hole and blow hard. The inside of the egg will drain from the larger hole.

Tie a knot in one end of a piece of ribbon. Thread the other end of the ribbon onto a large needle. Put the needle through the holes of the egg so that the knot is at the bottom of the egg. Remove the needle and tie a knot at the top of the egg. Hang your Pysanka egg and enjoy.

Activity: Easter Banner

Choose your favorite materials to make an Easter banner. Some of the options are felt and glue; scraps of material hand sewn; or special materials such as silk, wool, or velvet fully backed and hand sewn.

You will need:
    photocopies of symbols on pages 111-112
    and
    felt, glue
    or
    scraps of material, needle and thread
    or
    silk, wool, or velvet and backing; needle and thread

Use the symbols on pages 111 and 112 as patterns for your Easter banner, or design your own banner symbolizing what the Resurrection means to you.

The triangle with the three overlapping circles is a symbol of the Trinity—the Father, Son, and Holy Spirit. You might wish to use just a triangle or just the three overlapping circles as they are also symbols of the Trinity.

The butterfly is a symbol of new life. While the larva of a butterfly does not actually die, it does shed its chrysalis (former life) and live in a completely new state (butterfly), much like the resurrection of Christ enables us to claim new life and live in a completely new way.

The fish is a symbol of Christianity used by the first Christians to proclaim to each other their belief in the resurrected Christ.

The empty cross is the symbol that tells us that death did not win. Jesus died but was raised from the dead. He triumphed over the cross. The cross is the most common of the Resurrection symbols.

The crown is a symbol of the Lordship of Jesus Christ.

Other possible Resurrection symbols: a pomegranate, a peacock, a white lily, an egg, and a phoenix rising from the ashes.

Seasons of Faith

Seasons of Faith

Activity: Promise Butterflies

You will need:
- coffee filters
- watercolor markers
- chenille sticks
- mist bottle full of water
- old newspapers

Before you begin, spread out several layers of old newspaper on a table.

1. Use the watercolor markers to color one of the coffee filters. You may want to use just one color or several colors. This will be the butterfly's wings.

2. Mist the colored coffee filter lightly with water and set it out to dry.

3. Choose a chenille stick. This will be the body and antenna of your butterfly.

1.

4. Find the middle of your dried colored coffee filter and gently gather it together (not too tightly, because you want there to be some "body" to your butterfly).

5. Wrap the chenille stick around the gathered center and twist it together to hold the butterfly in place. Leave plenty of chenille stick at the top to make the butterfly's antennas.

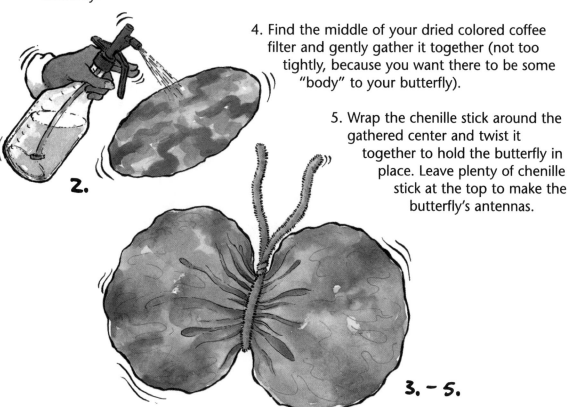

2.

3. – 5.

Activity: Scrambled Eggs

You will need:
   Bibles
   photocopy of page 115
   scissors
   sixty colored plastic eggs in six colors, ten eggs per color

Before the session, photocopy the six Scriptures on page 115. Cut each Scripture into ten phrases. The phrases are already divided for you. Simply look for the / marks.

Put all of the strips for one passage of Scripture in the same color eggs, one slip per egg. Hide the eggs around the room or outside.

Depending on the number of participants, the participants may work individually or they may work in six teams. Assign each team one color of eggs to find. When they have found all ten eggs in their color, they are to open the eggs, remove the slips, and work together to put the verse in order. They may use the Scripture reference on one of the slips to check their work in the Bible.

Once all of the teams have put their verses together, have them read the verses aloud.

Together discuss for each verse the following questions:
• What would you have thought if you had been there?
• What do you think you would have done?

Scrambled Egg Verses

Early on the first day of the /
week, while it was still /
dark, Mary Magdalene came to the tomb /
and saw that the stone had been /
removed from/
the tomb. So she ran and went to /
Simon Peter and [John]…and said /
to them, "They have taken the Lord out /
of the tomb, and we do not /
know where they have laid him."
(John 20:1-2)

But Thomas (who was called the Twin), /
one of the twelve, was not with /
them when Jesus came. So the other /
disciples told him, "We have seen /
the Lord." But he said to them, "Unless I /
see the mark of the nails /
in his hands, and put my finger /
in the mark of the nails and /
my hand in his side, I will /
not believe." (John 20:24-25)

**After the sabbath, as the first day of
the week was dawning, /
Mary Magdalene and the other Mary
went /
to see the tomb. And suddenly there
was a great/
earthquake; for an angel of the Lord,
descending from /
heaven, came and rolled back the
stone….His appearance was like /
lightning, and his clothing white as
snow. For fear of him the guards /
shook….But the angel said to the
women, "Do not /
be afraid; I know that you are looking
for /
Jesus who was crucified. He is not /
here; for he has been raised."
(Matthew 28:1-6)**

**But on the first day of the week, at
early dawn, they came to the tomb,
taking the spices that /
they had prepared. They found the
stone /
rolled away from the tomb, but /
when they went in, they did not find /
the body. While they were perplexed
about this, suddenly two men /
in dazzling clothes stood beside them. /
The women were terrified and bowed
their faces to the /
ground, but the men said to them,
"Why do you look for the living /
among the dead? He is not here, /
but has risen." (Luke 24:1-5)**

But Mary stood weeping outside/
the tomb. As she wept, she /
bent over to look into the tomb; /
and she saw two angels in white, sitting /
where the body of Jesus had /
been lying.…They said to her, /
"Woman, why are you /
weeping?" She said to them, "They have taken /
away my Lord, and I do not know /
where they have laid him." (John 20:11-13)

When it was evening on /
that day, the first day of /
the week, and the doors /
of the house where the /
disciples had met were /
locked for fear of the Jews, /
Jesus came and stood among /
them and said, "Peace /
be with you."…"As the Father has sent /
me, so I send you." (John 20:19-21)

Seasons of Faith

Activity: Easter Flowers

Making colorful paper flowers for celebrations is a Latin American tradition. If you do not have real flowers to place on an empty cross, make colorful paper flowers to place on an empty cross to symbolize the new life promised by Jesus' resurrection.

You will need:
> cross
> one, two, or three colors of tissue paper
> chenille sticks
> scissors

One way to make paper flowers:

1. Cut the tissue paper into strips (the wider and longer the strips, the bigger the flower). Stack three strips together.

2. Fold the paper accordion style and twist it together in the middle

3. Wrap a chenille stick around the middle to hold it together. Twist the chenille stick to make a flower stem.

4. Separate the layers of tissue paper.

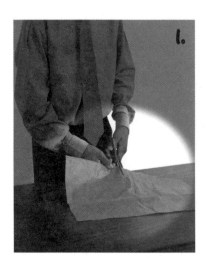

Ascension Sunday

Ascension Sunday

Ascension Day is considered to be a Thursday (the fortieth day of the Easter season). However, in churches the Ascension is usually celebrated on a Sunday—the Sunday following Ascension Day.

The celebration itself marks the Ascension of our Lord to heaven where he now sits at the right hand of God. This day reminds us of the true power and glory of Jesus, the crucified and resurrected Lord.

This day ties the Resurrection and the Ascension together.

Biblical references for the Ascension are Mark 16:19-20; Luke 24:50-53; and Acts 1:6-11.

Activity: Straw and Modeling clay

You will need:
   straw
   modeling clay
   children's building set (optional)

Place several straws and modeling clay on tables. (Another option would be to use any type of children's building set.)

Divide the participants into groups. Have each group build a Resurrection symbol for worship. They do not have to use any of the customary symbols; the more original they make their symbol, the better. They need to be ready to explain what their symbol means at worship.

Note: If you have a small class, let them work together as a class to create a symbol.

At the beginning of your closing worship, ask each group (or a representative from each group) to come forward and place their symbol on the worship table, then explain the meaning of their symbol.

Note: This activity will help your group learn to work together and will help them think about what the Resurrection means to them personally.

Activity: Study Creeds

The Ascension brings up the question for many people of what exactly they believe and how they can put their beliefs into words. One way to help them is to look at creeds. Most churches have access to the Apostles' Creed and the Nicene Creed, but there are also some modern creeds that express basic Christian beliefs in more modern and more readily understood language.

You will need:
> worship resources containing creeds
> large sheets of paper and markers

Ask your pastor to help you find some creeds. Most denominations have worship resources containing creeds. Take a large sheet of paper for each creed and write the creed out so that everyone can see. Post them in a prominent place.

Together talk about what the creeds mean. Divide the participants into groups and let them work together on writing their own creed. Encourage them to make their creeds short and very basic—things on which they can all agree.

Give each group a large sheet of paper on which to write their own creed. Post all of the new creeds for everyone to see.

Activity: The Ascension in Art

You will need:
> Bibles
> construction paper and markers
> art paper and water colors
> writing paper and pencils
> large sheets of paper and tempera paints
> modeling clay
> other craft items

Ask three participants to read aloud the different accounts of the ascension of Jesus: Mark 16:19-20; Luke 24:50-53; Acts 1:6-11.

Ask each participant to use whatever art form they wish to depict the ascension of Jesus. They can be literal about their interpretation, or they might want to be abstract. They might want to write about or depict their own feelings when they hear or read this story, or perhaps they want to depict the story from the point of view of one of the disciples.

When they have finished set up a display of their art and/or writings.

Note: Perhaps you have some drama buffs who would like to do their depiction through drama. Let them work together and then present their drama. If you have a musical person, they might want to write a song or select a relevant hymn to sing.

Pentecost

Pentecost

The last day of the Easter season is Pentecost. Pentecost is the second most important holiday for Christians. Easter, of course, celebrates the Resurrection. Pentecost celebrates the coming of the Holy Spirit on the disciples, empowering them to carry the Word of God to others. We celebrate Pentecost as the birthday of the church.

Actually Pentecost was originally a Jewish celebration—an agricultural festival celebrating the harvest. In Jesus' day it was customary for Jews to take the first fruits of their harvest to the Temple as an offering. This holiday for the Jews came to center on the giving of the Torah (the law of Moses). The reading of the Scriptures was a large part of the celebration.

To Christians Pentecost means the coming of the Holy Spirit—the birthday of the church.

After the ascension of Jesus, the disciples gathered once again in Jerusalem for the celebration of Pentecost. This is where Acts 2 begins. The story of the birth of the church is full of drama; sights and sounds abound. It is a joyous occasion.

Pentecost comes fifty days after Easter. This date was well-established by the third century.

The core of the Christian Year—the central message of the passion, resurrection, and ascension of Christ and the coming of the Holy Spirit—begins with Ash Wednesday and ends with Pentecost.

Activity: Pentecost Picnic

Pentecost falls in May or June each year (see the calendar on page 10 for dates of upcoming Pentecost days). This is a perfect time of year for a picnic, and Pentecost provides the perfect time to celebrate the coming of the Holy Spirit, the birthday of the church.

Have a picnic and spread out a red plastic tablecloth (see the Colors of the Christian Year chart on page 9—red is the color of Pentecost). Use red cups, red napkins, and red plastic utensils.

A week or two before the picnic make Pentecost Pennants (see pages 126 and 128) and attach them to the picnic table or the picnic shelter (or both) to let other picnickers know this is a special event. Have children in the church make Pentecost Pinwheels (pages 124 and 125) to hand out at the picnic.

Invite church members to the local park (or the church lawn if you have one) for a picnic after the morning worship service (never instead of the service, unless you have someone to hold the service outside—Pentecost Sunday is too important not to worship).

Fly kites; wind is one of the most powerful symbols of Pentecost. Read the story of Pentecost (Acts 2), then have a few kites on hand and let everyone take turns flying a kite (or attempting to fly one).

Play games and have a good time. This is a time for rejoicing—play relay games, water games, ball games; they do not have to have any special meaning other than a time for the family of God to come together and rejoice.

Before everyone leaves have birthday cake (it is the church's birthday) and have a short closing worship service.

Make it a Pentecost to remember.

If it rains, move it indoors. You will have to forgo kite flying, but you can make and play with Pentecost Pinwheels inside.

Activity: Pentecost Pinwheel

"And suddenly from heaven there came a sound like the rush of a violent wind, and it filled the entire house where they were sitting" (Acts 2:2).

Wind is one of the symbols of Pentecost. Make a symbolic pinwheel to remind you of the sound of violent wind at Pentecost.

Note: If you have young children, they may just color their pinwheel. Older children, youth, and adults can freehand draw the symbols of Pentecost (the seven-tongued flame and the descending dove).

You will need:
    photocopies of pattern (see p. 125)
    paper
    scissors
    crayons or markers
    pencils with erasers
    pushpins or tacks

1. On a piece of paper, make a square with lines and a circle in the middle as is shown in the pattern on page 125.

2. Decorate the square using flames or a descending dove. The color of Pentecost is red so you will probably want to use that color somehow. Be creative; your pinwheel should look the way you want it to look.

3. Cut out the square. Then cut along the solid lines toward the center. Be careful not to cut into the middle circle.

4. Fold the points of the square along the dotted lines into the center.

5. Push a pin (one with a big head) or a tack through the center being sure to catch each point in the pin or tack. Then push the pin or tack into a pencil eraser. The eraser protects you and others from the sharp tip of the pin or tack, and the pencil becomes your holder for the pinwheel.

6. Open the spaces where the points are folded down so that air can get in.

Note: This pinwheel is manually operated. You will need to blow (or stand outside in a good breeze) to make it spin.

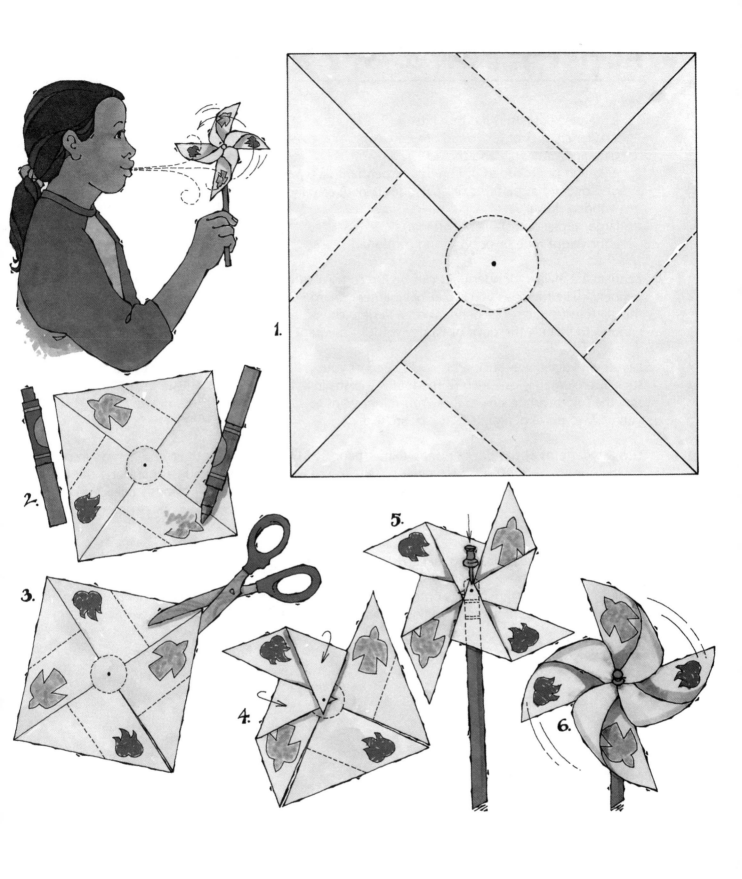

1.

2.

3.

4.

5.

6.

Activity: Pentecost Pennants

You will need:

> large piece of felt in red or white
> smaller squares of felt in red or white (opposite color of large piece of felt)
> glue and/or needle and thread
> enlarged photocopies of patterns of pennant (see page 127)
> photocopies of patterns of dove and flame (see page 128)
> wooden dowel
> large stapler and staples (optional)
> lightweight rope or heavy string (optional)

Banners are always wonderful; it can be fun to try a variation of a banner—that is, a pennant—like the ones you see at ball games. Enlarge the pennant pattern on page 127. Use this pattern to trace your pennant on a large piece of felt. (Make sure your pennant is large enough to include the dove or flame symbol—see page 128.)

Lay down your dowel stick on the wide end of your pennant. Fold the pennant over the dowel stick approximately one inch (if the fold is too shallow it puts a strain on the seam). Glue or sew the fold over the dowel stick. You might want to staple the felt to the dowel at one end if you wish to make pennants that can be held.

Use the patterns of the dove and the flame (page 128) to cut out the dove and flame symbols on the opposite color from the pennant itself. You may do a single-sided pennant or a double-sided one. You may glue your symbols onto one side of the pennant or to both sides. You may wish to sew your symbols onto your pennant, or you may want to make your pennant itself a double thickness and sew it together to make it stronger.

You may wish to add the word *Pentecost* to your pennant in some manner.

Option: String several pennants onto a lightweight rope or a heavy string and hang them in large rows like you might see hanging in front of a car lot.

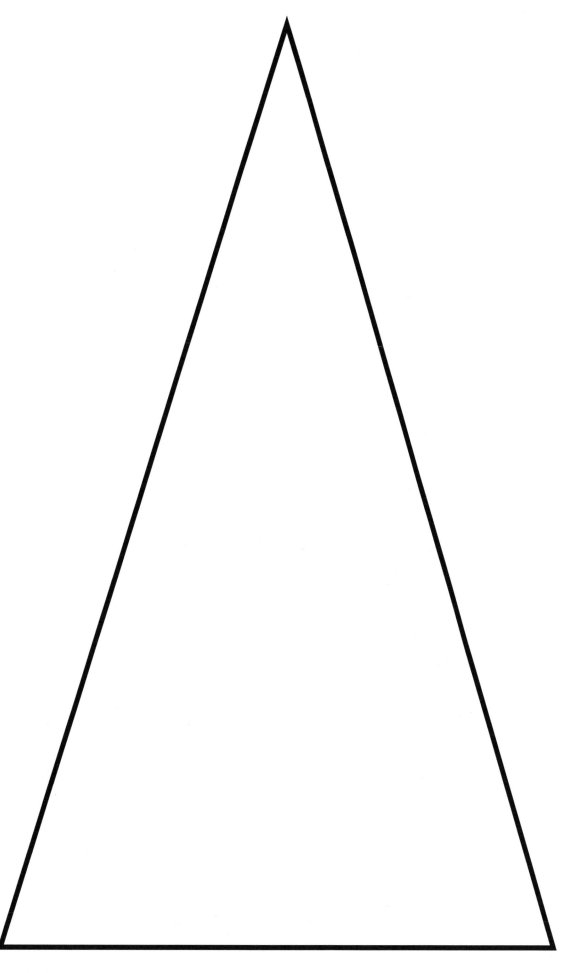

Seasons of Faith

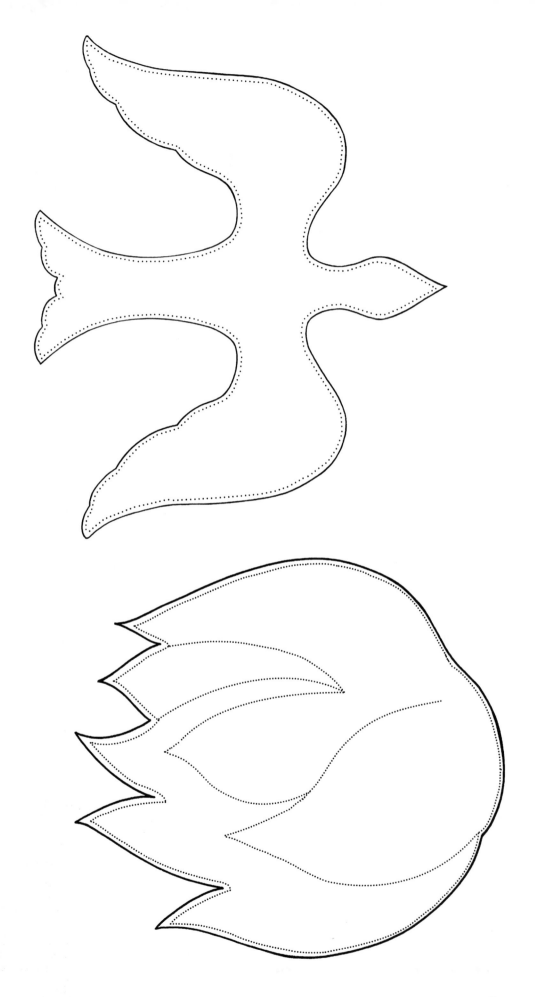

Seasons of Faith

Season After Pentecost

Days After Pentecost

The Season After Pentecost is the longest season of the Christian Year. Other terms for it are Ordinary Time and Kingdomtide. The color for this season is green.

The following days are those that fall in the Season After Pentecost:

Trinity Sunday—the first Sunday after Pentecost
Second Sunday after Pentecost to the Twenty-sixth Sunday After Pentecost (each Sunday after Pentecost and Easter is numbered in its relationship to Pentecost)
World Communion Sunday—the first Sunday of October
All Saints Day
Christ the King Sunday (sometimes called the Reign of Christ Sunday)—this is the last Sunday after Pentecost

The Church Year cycle then begins again with the first Sunday of Advent.

Note: Thanksgiving is usually celebrated officially by most churches the Sunday before Thanksgiving, though some celebrate it the Sunday after Thanksgiving. In this book it is included in Other Celebrations (see page 144).

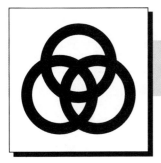

Trinity Sunday

Trinity Sunday is the first Sunday after Pentecost. It is a transitional Sunday. It takes us from the Season of Lent/Easter/Pentecost into a season called Ordinary Time. (Another term for this time is Kingdomtide.) Trinity Sunday gives us the opportunity to celebrate the Holy Trinity, the three natures of God: the Father, the Son, and the Holy Spirit.

The concept of the Holy Trinity is difficult to understand and is mysterious even to the most learned biblical scholar. The Trinity is core to Christian belief.

Complete understanding of the Trinity is not imperative to believing in it. We often believe in things that most of us don't understand completely—air waves bouncing sound out to a satellite in space which then bounces it back somewhere else, the GNP (Gross National Product), and a mother's love for her child.

Few take the time to scientifically explain a mother's love for her child, but we all understand it on some level. The understanding differs depending upon our relationship with our mothers. The same is true with our relationship with the Trinity; our understanding often depends upon our own individual spiritual journey.

The Trinity is the Christian way of explaining the three ways we see God acting in the world: the Father, the creator; the Son, God come down to us in our human, everyday lives; the Holy Spirit, the spiritual element of the Trinity.

Trinity Sunday is the day that we celebrate this Great Mystery.

Symbols of the Trinity are very important in Christianity. Some of the symbols for the Trinity are:

Three Entwined Circles | The Circle and The Triangle | The Iris | The Shamrock | The Triquetra | The Equilateral Triangle

Activity: Celebrate With Symbols

Instead of trying to explain the Trinity, allow symbols of the Trinity to do the explaining for you.

Have members of a group or the congregation come together before Trinity Sunday worship to make all sorts of symbols to hang, post, and/or hand out all over the church. Surround worshipers with images of the Trinity. For patterns enlarge the images on page 131 or use the patterns from *Symbols of Faith*, published by Abingdon Press.

Some suggestions:

• Trinity bulletin board

• Banners for the sanctuary

• Pennants on a rope to drape down hallways and/or across the entrance doors

• Trinity buttons made with a button-making kit (hand draw and color the symbols to go on the buttons)

• Nametags for ushers and/or congregants with Trinity symbols drawn on them

• Index card with a Trinity symbol on it and a short explanation of the meaning (hand these out with the worship bulletins)

• Bulletin covers that have a Trinity symbol on the cover

• Three large hula hoops tied together to make entwined circles and hung from the ceiling of the sanctuary

Seasons of Faith

World Communion Sunday

World Communion Sunday is celebrated on the first Sunday in October. All Christian congregations around the world are asked to celebrate the sacrament of Holy Communion on this day. This is a day which is designated for the church to be openly and symbolically universal. Churches that celebrate Communion only monthly, quarterly, or on special days find this day especially important.

World Communion Sunday was first celebrated by the Presbyterian Church in 1936. It was adopted by the Federal Council of Churches in 1940. Other denominations have adopted this day also.

The day is celebrated simply as its name states—by churches celebrating Communion during their times of worship. Often the global nature of the church is celebrated in Sunday schools on this day.

Activity: Dinner Around the World

World Communion Sunday is the perfect time to make connections to Christians of every place and culture. Why not make this a special time by having "dinner around the world"?

On the evening of World Communion Sunday gather for dinner. Ahead of time designate tables to represent different countries and/or cultures. You can do this one of several ways.

Option 1: Designate each dining table as a different "country." Have the tables decorated with things representing the designated country. Have someone responsible for providing a meal from that country. People may sign up to sit at the table representing the country of their choice (to accommodate everyone make sure they also specify a second and third choice).

Option 2: Set up tables around the edge of the room for display. Ask people from the congregation to sign up to decorate a specific table with items from their chosen country. Then ask each person who signed up for a table to please bring a dish from that country to be part of an international potluck dinner. There are many recipes available on the Internet or, if you have an international market in your area, they have authentic items for you to prepare.

Variation: If you are lucky enough to have several cultures represented by the members of your congregation, encourage people to sign up to decorate a table and provide authentic food from their own cultures. Then encourage everyone to experience a culture other than their own.

Program option: Have books or Internet information available for each country and let the people at the table discover some information about their chosen country. Let the people at the table decide how they would like to present the information to the other tables—they can do a skit, just tell some interesting facts, or create a "pop" quiz to see what people know about their assigned country. If people who have a connection to these countries are available, they could teach a song from their culture, or teach people to say "welcome" in the language of the country, and so forth.

Activity: World Communion Service Project

Celebrate World Communion Sunday by taking Communion to persons who are homeless.

For persons who are homeless many things that the rest of us take for granted are often unavailable. Souls suffer as well as bodies and self-esteem. Make arrangements with a homeless shelter to take Communion to persons who are homeless.

• Ask the pastor to lead the group that will take the Communion or to bless the Communion elements that you will take to serve.

• Make arrangements in advance with the homeless shelter. You will need an area where you can hold a short Communion service and serve the elements. Remember that not all persons who are homeless are Christians and participation will be strictly voluntary.

• Partake in Communion along with persons who are homeless. This makes them part of the Christian community as a whole instead of just recipients of a charitable act.

• Take along care packages to give to persons who are homeless when you leave. A small plastic container that can be carried in a pocket or a small bag with handles to hold items is helpful (they will have to carry it with them). Put in small portable items such as travel sizes of toothpaste, toothbrushes, deodorant, and so forth. If you have enough money and you can find small sizes, you might wish to give them pocket-size New Testaments.

All Hallows Eve

This day is most commonly called Halloween. It is the Eve of All Saints Day. Yes, a pagan holiday was incorporated into a new Christian celebration. All Hallows Eve and All Saints Day in Christian tradition are tied together. All Hallows Eve comes from All Hallows Day—Hallow meaning Holy. We now know All Hallows Day as All Saints Day. All Hallows Eve was the night before All Saints Day and became shortened to "Halloween." For the European Roman Catholic Church, All Hallows Eve had a much greater significance than it ever had for Protestants or for the United States.

The actual celebration of Halloween goes back to the ancient Celts and a celebration held on October 31. It was a pagan celebration whose day was taken over by the church and remolded to fit its own purposes. Over the years the actual celebration of the day in the United States has become an entirely non-Christian holiday—a time for children to go "trick or treating," gathering candy, dressing up in outlandish costumes, and trying to find ways to scare themselves and each other.

All Hallows Eve is not often celebrated as a part of the Christian Year for most churches anymore, but many churches are attempting to find a way to have a celebration on this day that will lead children away from witches and ghosts—a way to counteract the popular culture's fascination with this holiday. (It is second only to Christmas in retail sales.)

Note: *All Hallows Eve is included in this section of the book due to its relationship with All Saints Day.*

Activity: All Hallows Eve Party

If you are looking for a Christian alternative to the usual Halloween activities, your church might try an All Hallows Eve party. Let preteen Sunday school classes, youth groups, or adult Sunday school classes use this party as a fundraiser (or a service to the church).

At the beginning of October hand out information on some famous Christians (people like Mother Teresa, Joan of Arc, and so forth). Issue an open invitation to the congregation to come to an All Hallows Eve party dressed as their favorite Bible character (Jesus should not be portrayed this way), as a famous Christian, or as someone who has been a Christian example to them.

At the party:
- Do a lot of the things you would do at a Halloween party: bob for apples, have a parade, give prizes for costumes, have a cake-walk, and so forth.

- Set up games for the children for which tickets can be purchased (money going to missions); if the service project is the party itself, then the games can be played for free.

- Do not strain too hard to work this party into the "Christian" experience mold. The main objective is to provide an alternative to the normal Halloween events (and to provide the children with a really good time).

For Youth and Adults: This event could be modified to be a great party for youth and/or adults. Challenge each member of the group to devise a costume to fit one of three categories: biblical costume, historical or modern Christian person, or a Christian symbol (for example, someone could choose to come as a fish).

Encourage research before this class event. Ask everyone to explain his or her costume. Give prizes for the most creative, the most authentic, and the funniest costumes.

Enjoy snacks and fellowship.

All Saints Day

November 1 is All Saints Day; it is a Christian day of remembrance. The day is often celebrated by the church on the first Sunday of November if All Saints Day does not fall on Sunday.

In the modern Protestant Church the saints being celebrated are all Christian people of every time and place. One of the Scriptures for this day is Hebrews 12:1, "Therefore, since we are surrounded by so great a cloud of witnesses, let us also lay aside every weight and the sin that clings so closely, and let us run with perseverance the race that is set before us."

Many churches use this Sunday to read a list of those who have died during the past year. Some churches have processionals with banners listing the names of those who have died in the past year.

Some churches also read listings of those baptized and taken into church membership during the year.

Activity: All Saints Service Project

Since All Saints Day commemorates the saints of the church you might want to participate in a service project that reflects the meaning of the day. Here are some suggestions:

- Create a memorial garden. If your church has a small spot that needs landscaping, suggest a memorial garden. Place a plaque in the garden naming the saints that have died during the year. Names could be added each year.

- Donate trees to your town or city to be planted where needed. Give one for each of the saints from your church who have died in the past year.

- Sponsor a party for everyone in the church. An important part of this party will be to invite and provide transportation for those who cannot or should not drive (this list will expand if the event is held at night). At some point a rousing rendition of "When the Saints Go Marching In" should be played and sung.

- Collect money to give as extra giving to a missionary from your local congregation. This should be above and beyond the usual donations.

- Together talk about some of the mission and/or service projects that are of special importance to the "saints" in your group. Let them decide to which mission and/or service project they want to dedicate themselves for the next year, then spend the year working on this project. At the end of the year have a party celebrating what they have accomplished.

Activity: Creating a Saints Memorial

Create a memorial to the saints in your church. You can make a triptych memorial to be set on a table in a foyer, displayed on a bulletin board, or set on the worship table of your sanctuary (if the memorial is large enough).

You may let each person make his or her own "memorial" or you may let the group work together to make a group memorial for church display and/or use.

You will need:
- photocopy of triptych (see page 141)
- crayons
- cotton balls
- posterboard
- paint and paintbrushes (optional)
- black felt-tip marker
- newspapers
- baby oil or vegetable oil
- scissors

A triptych is a set of three panels that can be hinged together (or more simply folded) so that the three panels can stand freely.

- Make a photocopy of the triptych on page 141. If you wish to make a large triptych, you will need to enlarge the copy.

- First have the participants write the names of those from your congregation who have died this year in heavy black felt-tip marker on the three panels. (Or your participants may wish to honor those saints to whom they are related who have died in recent years.)

- Have participants color the rest of the triptych pattern using crayons. The heavier the color, the more gloss you will get to the finished product.

- Spread newspapers out on a table and have them rub baby oil or vegetable oil on the back of the triptych using cotton balls. Let this dry completely.

- While it is drying have the participants make a frame for their triptych (much like a folding screen) out of posterboard. If they like they can paint this frame any color they wish. Be sure that the center of the frame is cut out so that when you glue the "stained-glass" triptych to the back of the frame the complete front of the triptych can be seen. Set this in front of a window where light will shine through.

Variation 1: Use the triptych pattern on page 141 to trace the design onto clear plastic. Paint the outline of the triptych with 3-D paints. Cut the plastic to the shape of the triptych pattern. Don't forget to add the names of the saints.

Variation 2: If you have someone in your congregation who is good with woodworking, have them make you a triptych board (again it will be like a folding screen only the panels will need to be hinged to fold toward the center). Either freestyle or by using the pattern on page 141 as a guide, use paints to paint your triptych, remembering to paint in the name of the saints you are memorializing.

Christ the King Sunday

Christ the King Sunday is the last Sunday of the Christian Year. Christ the King Sunday is usually considered a transitional Sunday, taking us from Ordinary Time into the beginning of the next Christian Year—the Advent season.

This Sunday usually falls the Sunday before Thanksgiving, although it can occasionally coincide with the Sunday after Thanksgiving. (Christ the King Sunday can fall anywhere from November 20 through November 26. Thanksgiving can fall anywhere from November 22 to November 28.)

Christ the King Sunday is not usually observed as a large celebration, since most people are focused on Thanksgiving and the beginning of Advent. However, this is a good time to concentrate on Christ as King as it sets the tone for Advent—the birth of the King—and is also appropriate when combined with thankfulness for what God has given to us.

Other Celebrations

Thanksgiving Day

Most of us know the history of the American Thanksgiving Day—the hard winter endured by the Pilgrims their first year in Plymouth and the celebration of the harvest. It was not a straight path to the day we know today, but the history books are full of explanations.

In 1863 President Abraham Lincoln proclaimed the last Thursday in November as a national day of Thanksgiving. If you have never read this proclamation, read it now on page 145. It is a remarkable document, written in wartime, full of praise and thanksgiving to God for what was good even in a time of national crisis.

The timing of Thanksgiving Day has been changed over the years, but finally in 1941 Congress made Thanksgiving an official holiday on the fourth Thursday in November.

Churches today in the United States usually have a Thanksgiving celebration in their regular Sunday morning worship service, giving thanks to God for their abundance.

Thanksgiving is often a time in churches of food drives for the hungry and discussions in Sunday school classes about what we have to be thankful for.

Thanksgiving Proclamation

The year that is drawing toward its close has been filled with the blessings of fruitful fields and healthful skies. To these bounties, which are so constantly enjoyed that we are prone to forget the source from which they come, others have been added which are of so extraordinary a nature that they can not fail to penetrate and soften even the heart which is habitually insensible to the ever-watchful providence of Almighty God.

In the midst of a civil war of unequaled magnitude and severity, which has sometimes seemed to foreign states to invite and to provoke their aggression, peace has been preserved with all nations, order has been maintained, the laws have been respected and obeyed, and harmony has prevailed everywhere, except in the theater of military conflict, while that theater has been greatly contracted by the advancing armies and navies of the Union.

Needful diversions of wealth and of strength from the fields of peaceful industry to the national defense have not arrested the plow, the shuttle, or the ship; the ax has enlarged the borders of our settlements, and the mines, as well of iron and coal as of the precious metals, have yielded even more abundantly than heretofore. Population has steadily increased notwithstanding the waste that has been made in the camp, the siege, and the battlefield, and the country, rejoicing in the consciousness of augmented strength and vigor, is permitted to expect continuance of years with large increase of freedom.

No human counsel hath devised nor hath any mortal hand worked out these great things. They are the gracious gifts of the Most High God, who, while dealing with us in anger for our sins, hath nevertheless remembered mercy.

It has seemed to me fit and proper that they should be solemnly, reverently, and gratefully acknowledged, as with one heart and one voice, by the whole American people. I do therefore invite my fellow-citizens in every part of the United States, and also those who are at sea and those who are sojourning in foreign lands, to set apart and observe the last Thursday of November next as a day of thanksgiving and praise to our beneficent Father who dwelleth in the heavens. And I recommend to them that while offering up the ascriptions justly due to Him for such singular deliverances and blessings they do also, with humble penitence for our national perverseness and disobedience, commend to His tender care all those who have become widows, orphans, mourners, or sufferers in the lamentable civil strife in which we are unavoidably engaged, and fervently implore the interposition of the Almighty hand to heal the wounds of the nation and to restore it, as soon as may be consistent with the divine purposes, to the full enjoyment of peace, harmony, tranquility, and union.

Abraham Lincoln
October 3, 1863

Activity: Song Search

You will need:
>   hymnals
>   song books
>   contemporary CDs (those with lyrics on the CD jacket)
>   large sheets of paper
>   markers

Divide into groups. Give each group a set of whatever resources you have gathered. Set a time limit depending on your program time. Have them search the resources for thankful songs.

Each group must list their songs on their large sheet of paper. The groups are racing to see who can list the most songs. Each group gets to decide how their team will work together as a group. (Give them a couple of minutes to decide this before you begin the timed activity.)

When you call time, each group is to stop. Have them post their findings and compare their lists.

Scoring: One point for each hymn or song listed.
>   Minus one point if they have listed any hymn or song twice or if it has no thankful message.
>   Five bonus points if they are the ONLY group to list a particular song or hymn.
>   Five bonus points if they have the most songs or hymns listed.
>   Five bonus points for the team that comes up with the most creative listing.
>   Ten bonus points for any group picking a song or hymn and singing it together for the others.

Hint: The words *thankful* or *thanks* do not have to appear in the song. For example: "Blessed Assurance" is a thankful song. It speaks of the "blessedness" of the assurance of having Jesus as Savior. That certainly is thankful.

Have a judge or a panel of judges who will make determinations in case of disputes.

Note: You might want to give bonus points if a group comes up with a truly original explanation for why an "iffy" choice is thankful.

Activity: Thankful Service

A thankful service is one that is inspired by that for which the group is thankful.

You will need:
    large sheet of paper
    markers

Post a large sheet of paper. As participants arrive, have them use a marker to write on the paper two things for which they are really thankful. It must be something different than the things that those arriving before them have written.

After everyone has gathered have them look at the list. Together walk them through a process of deciding what things they are thankful for that they can turn into a service project.

Some will be easy:

> If they are thankful for food, they can do a food drive for the local food bank.

> If they are thankful for a warm home, they might want to help with a Habitat for Humanity project.

These are good things, but also encourage them to think creatively:

> If someone is thankful for computers, maybe they can collect all their used computer games and donate them to an organization such as the local library or to a community center that gives out such things at Christmas.

> If someone is thankful for all the trees that bloom in the spring, perhaps you might choose to plant trees on Arbor Day.

> If someone is thankful for such critters as snakes, spiders, and alligators, have a fund drive and donate some money to the local zoo.

Let them brainstorm service projects large and small, sensible and crazy. Then (within sensible parameters) have the group narrow the list to one or two service projects. Together plan the projects completely, assigning tasks and dates by which certain things must be done—gathering information, advertising, raising funds, finishing the project).

Then go ahead and do your thankful service project.

St. Valentine's Day

The true origins of St. Valentine's Day are confusing and often contradictory. In fact, it has been so confusing that the Roman Catholic Church has dropped it as an official celebration. It has never been an official Christian holiday in the Protestant Church.

It seems that the Roman Catholic Church has at least three saints named Valentine or Valenitinus. It is said that they were all martyred on February 14. But many believe that the holiday itself has its roots in a very unsavory pagan holiday that the church wished to change.

Despite its origins (go to the Internet and type in "Valentine's Day" and "history" and you'll find all kinds of web sites) or its meanings, many people love Valentine's Day, especially retailers. Valentine's Day can also be a very painful day for those who have lost a loved one, or perhaps just have no one special in their lives at the time.

There are some ways to celebrate Valentine's Day to make the celebration a little more meaningful for all and perhaps a little less painful for those who find these kinds of holidays especially lonely.

Pages 149 and 150 give you just two ideas. If you put your imagination to work you can probably come up with many more ways to add a little Christian love and charity to February 14.

Activity: Secret Valentine Project

Gather the names and addresses of people in your church who might need cheering up or just a little extra attention. Sometimes Valentine's Day can be difficult on people who have lost loved ones, people who live alone and do not have a "sweetheart," people who are sick, college students in other states, or anyone who has had a difficult year.

This year have a Secret Valentine Project to bring a little extra sunshine into the lives of some of these people. Take the names you have gathered and put them in a basket or some sort of container and let everyone in your group draw one or more names until all of the names are gone.

As a group brainstorm some things that would bring a smile to the person(s) chosen to be your secret valentines.

You can make cards and mail them to your valentines. You can choose to anonymously do something nice for your valentines, like shovel snow off their sidewalk or wash their car. You might want to put flowers on the altar on the Sunday closest to Valentine's Day in honor of a personal secret valentine or the entire group of secret valentines.

You could choose the whole month of February to do something special—something each week, or something each day, or three or four times during the month.

You might wish to invite all of the secret valentines to a special tea or dinner close to Valentine's Day to reveal who their secret pal is, or you may simply wish to keep it a secret and let them continue to wonder.

Use your imaginations. Do fun, thoughtful things. Don't go overboard spending money. The purpose of this project is not to help the retailers make money on candy and flowers but to spread a little joy and some good Christian love.

Activity: Valentine Dinner Fundraiser

Want to make some money for your favorite missions project? Hold a Valentine Dinner and charge admission.

Caution: This is hard work!

Invite the entire congregation to make reservations to come to a dinner held at your church on Valentine's Day.

You will need active participation of every person in your group. (If you are working with preteens and/or youth only, you will also need to enlist the help of adults.)

List things that need to be done to put on an elegant Valentine's Day dinner.

Menu (what will you serve?)

Food (try to get all or some of it donated)

Cooks (somebody has to cook the meal)

Tables (set up and take down)

Decorations

Food Servers

Tickets and Ticket Takers

Advertising

Clean Up

Make sure that everyone has an assignment. One church I know set up their fellowship hall as a restaurant with tables for two, four (or three), six, and a couple of large ones in case families or groups of singles wished to sit together. The meal was served by reservations only.

Lights were dimmed and the "restaurant" was decorated with real tablecloths, vases with flowers, and other decorative touches (they used card tables except for the tables for larger groups). Soft music was played, you gave your ticket at a table at the entrance, a rose was handed to every woman who came, and you were escorted to your table (reservations were set for two different times so that each table could be used twice). Your server (dressed in a suit or a dressy dress) came to your table and took your order for water, tea, or coffee and your choice of salad dressing. Everything else was a standard menu. Dessert was served.

An area in one corner was set up where you could choose to have your picture taken with your "sweetheart" or as a group. Then you could purchase your picture for a set price (picture to be delivered later).

A wonderful time was had by everyone who attended the dinner, and the money went to a youth mission project.

St. Patrick's Day

Don't we hear it every year on March 17?—On St. Patrick's Day everybody is Irish. People wear green, shamrock plants are sold, and Chicago puts green dye in the river. One church even served green dye in all of its food for Wednesday night supper one year. (Very little food was actually eaten that night.)

Go to the Internet and discover a lot of wonderful stories about St. Patrick (some true, many mere legends) and the history of St. Patrick's Day.

St. Patrick was a true Saint of the Roman Catholic Church. He was not Irish but British, but he spent six years in captivity in Ireland. It was at this time that Patrick became a devout Christian (although they say Patrick may not even have been his true name).

In the United States St. Patrick's Day is not a holiday with any real religious connotation or celebration.

However, there is a wonderful story of St. Patrick explaining the Trinity to the King of Ireland that makes this day (or a Sunday close to it) a wonderful time to teach people about the Holy Trinity: Father, Son, and Holy Spirit.

This story has made the shamrock a symbol for the Trinity. The story is told on page 152.

Activity: Give Shamrocks

You will need:
- shamrock plants
- green foil to wrap plants
- green construction paper or white card stock
- pens or markers

Very few people think of doing service projects for St. Patrick's Day, so it can be a wonderful time to do something unexpected. Collect money or arrange with a local nursery to donate some shamrock plants in plastic containers. Wrap the plant containers in green foil paper.

Make a card to go with the plant. Copy by hand the story of the shamrock below onto green construction paper and fold the construction paper to make it into a card, or write the story on white card stock and decorate the card with green shamrocks.

Go in small groups to deliver your St. Patrick's Day pick-me-ups to members of the congregation who are ill.

The Story of the Shamrock

The shamrock is called the "Irish Shamrock" because not only is it found growing in Ireland, but one legend says that about four hundred years after Christ, a missionary named Patrick (later known as St. Patrick) came before the Irish king and explained the Trinity to him. But this only made the king angry and confused because he could not understand the idea of "three persons in one." Patrick bent down, picked a shamrock, and showed the king that one perfect leaf could have three perfect parts. The king could not explain whether the shamrock was one leaf or three, and that is how the king came to understand that something so complex and unbelievable could be true. From that day forward, the shamrock has been a symbol of the Trinity.

Seasons of Faith

Mother's Day

Mother's Day is always observed on the second Sunday in May. This is a day that honors all mothers. Anna Jarvis wanted to honor her mother, and so in May, 1907, the service to honor mothers was held at the Methodist Episcopal Church in Grafton, West Virginia.

By 1908 Anna Jarvis was trying to get the nation to support naming a day to celebrate mothers. The Methodist Episcopal Church got behind her to promote this holiday.

Today Mother's Day is celebrated by Christians in worship services around the country.

The United States is not the only country that has a day honoring mothers.

Father's Day

Father's Day is observed on the third Sunday of June.

The holiday began in 1910 when Sonara Dodd of Spokane, Washington, organized the first Father's Day celebration in her hometown.

In 1956 a Father's Day observance was recognized by a Joint Congressional Resolution. In 1966 President Lyndon Johnson issued a presidential proclamation declaring Father's Day an official holiday. In 1972 President Richard Nixon signed a law making the third Sunday of June the official day for the celebration of fathers.

Festival of the Christian Home

The United Methodist Church observes the second Sunday in May not only as Mother's Day but as the Festival of the Christian Home. The centrality of the Christian home in the life of Christians is recognized and honored on this day.

This celebration enhances the celebration of Mother's Day, emphasizing the importance of mothers to the Christian family.

Activity: Honoring those who Nurture Us

Mother's Day and Father's Day are wonderful celebrations. However, they are also often painful celebrations. Parents who have lost a child in an accident, to a war, or to disease often find these holidays painful. Children who have been orphaned can feel lonely on these days. Single men and women who have never had the opportunity to be a parent feel left out. And both parents and children from families where a divorce has occurred find these days difficult because custody issues and time with the other parent can cause conflicts.

So what is one way to celebrate these holidays and make them meaningful and joyful for all? Celebrate all of those who nurture us. It really does take a village (or at least a church family) to raise a child and to nurture that child in the Christian faith.

Mother's Day—Have children make paper flower corsages for all the women in the church age eighteen and older. Organize the children to pin the corsages on the women as they enter the worship service. Ask the pastor to recognize in the service the many ways all the women in the church nurture the children of the church.

Father's Day—Inexpensive, plain baseball caps can be purchased in bulk from a vendor such as S&S® (1-800-243-9232; www.ssww.com). Before Father's Day gather all of the children and have them decorate these baseball caps to give to the men at the church. Have the children hand them out as the men enter church. At the point when all the men in the service are to be honored, have them put on their hats and stand. This activity will be good for boys, especially when they see how many men are involved in the life of the church.

Activity: Make Church Family Memories

In this time of broken homes, blended families, single moms and dad, widows and widowers living alone, those who have chosen to remain single, grandparents in far away places, and so forth, it's difficult to do family-centered functions at church without excluding many people.

Take this year to concentrate on celebrating the church family and make memories of "family" for those who may be lacking extensive families.

Ideas to get you started:

- Have intergenerational special events. At these events do not divide people by biological families, but by other criteria, making certain that people from every age level are represented in each group and that singles and others are invited and feel equally welcome.

- Pair singles, older people whose grandchildren live far away, widowers, and so forth with preteens or youth for mentoring opportunities.

- Hold church picnics and celebrations that are centered on everyone, regardless of circumstances, feeling included.

- Hold an event honoring those who have nurtured and/or mentored your church members over the years. Even ten-year-olds know what adults have been important to them.

As people arrive give them each a piece of paper and let them list everyone they can remember who helped them or nurtured them. Then bring them together in groups. Give each group a large sheet of paper and some markers. Have them go over their lists together, and on their sheet of paper write the categories of adults who have been Christian family to them.

Some possibilities: relatives
                        teachers
                        Boy Scout/Girl Scout leaders
                        Vacation Bible School leaders
                        choir directors
                        the older people who gave them things (coins/candy)
                        the person who sent a birthday card every year

Bring all the groups together, go over the categories, then decide on a way to celebrate these people—hold a party, write thank-you notes, ask the minister to remember them in a special service, create a photo album, and so forth. You are limited only by your collective imaginations.

Activity: our Family Traditions

To celebrate the Festival of the Christian Home, honor family traditions.

As participants arrive play a couple of games that are traditional in your area—games that people probably already know how to play. Then serve refreshments; people are often more apt to talk while in a relaxed, friendly atmosphere.

This activity can be done as a group if there are only a few participants, but if there are more than ten participants divide up into smaller groups.

Name one holiday: Christmas, Easter, the Fourth of July, and so forth.

Ask each person in the group to tell the others in their group four things:
1. With whom do you celebrate this holiday?
2. What do you eat on this holiday?
3. Where do you celebrate this holiday?
4. What is one special thing you do on this holiday?

The only rule is that they must answer with what they and/or their families most often do.

If you are gathering to celebrate one particular holiday, end with discussing only that holiday. If you are coming together to talk about family traditions, give everyone time to talk about the holiday that was originally named; then name a different holiday, and have them go through the same four questions.

Bring everyone back together and ask the groups if all members in their group celebrate these holidays the same way or differently.

Pick a holiday and have each group decide on something from their "traditions" to do at this party—something special to eat, a particular outing (maybe one family does a tacky light tour at Christmas or always does an Advent worship), anything that comes up that is feasible to do at a party.

Index

REPRODUCIBLES

SERVICE PROJECTS

SPECIAL STUDIES

WORSHIP ENHANCEMENTS

CREDITS